Worship Him

Dr. Fuchsia Pickett

WORSHIP HIM by Fuchsia Pickett
Published by Creation House
A part of Strang Communications Company
600 Rinehart Road
Lake Mary, FL 32746
www.creationhouse.com

Unless otherwise noted, all Scripture quotations are from the
King James Version of the Bible.

Scripture quotations marked AMP are from the Amplified Bible,
Old Testament copyright © 1965, 1987 by the Zondervan
Corporation. The Amplified New Testament copyright © 1954,
1958, 1987 by the Lockman Foundation. Used by permission.

Scripture quotations marked NAS are from the New American
Standard Bible. Copyright © 1960, 1962, 1963, 1968, 1971, 1972,
1973, 1975, 1977 by the Lockman Foundation. Used by permission.

Scripture quotations marked NIV are from the Holy Bible, New
International Version. Copyright © 1973, 1978, 1984,
International Bible Society. Used by permission.

Library of Congress Cataloging-in-Publication Data:
Pickett, Fuchsia T.
    Worship him / by Fuchsia T. Pickett.
    p. cm.
    Includes bibliographical references.
    ISBN 0-88419-723-9
    1. Worship. 2. Worship in the Bible. I. Title.
    BV10.2.P54 2000   99-058696
    248.3–dc21

0 1 2 3 4 5 6 VERSA 8 7 6 5 4 3

Printed in the United States of America

Dedicated to:

My husband, Leroy, who is my faithful coworker, main support and encouragement—never letting me lose sight of our mandate from God.

And to:

My son, Darrell W. Parrish, Sr., with whom I share such precious fellowship and encouragement to fulfill the calling of God on my life.

These two will share whatever reward that awaits this unworthy but grateful servant of the Lord.

I want to acknowledge some precious people who have had such a rich influence in my life by both their example and teaching on pure spiritual worship:

— I saw and experienced the reality of real worship in the lives of Dr. Iona Glasier, Dr. Sam Sasser and Pastor Larry Dempsey—all three are now worshiping around the throne.

— Also, my friends Dr. Judson Cornwall and Dr. Charlotte Baker, who are wonderful teachers and leaders of worship in the body of Christ today. They made me desperately hungry years ago to be not a spectator, but a real participant in pure spiritual worship.

— And my administrator, Carol Noe, who not only insisted that my notes on worship needed to be published, but who also worked hard compiling them into manuscript form to see this goal accomplished.

Contents

The Priority of Worship

The Heart of the Worshiper

SHORTLY AFTER I WAS HEALED FROM A LIFE-THREATENING disease and baptized in the Holy Spirit, I was asked to minister in a Pentecostal church. There I was introduced to a dimension of worship that I had never experienced before. Sitting on the platform in my studied dignity as a former Methodist professor, observing the worship service that was so different from that to which I was accustomed, I was fascinated by all that was going on around me. Though their worship expression seemed disorderly—almost irreverent—in comparison with Methodist tradition, I could tell these people deeply loved the Lord and were expressing their love to Him.

I looked down from my seat on the platform and saw a pretty redheaded woman standing with her hands raised and her eyes closed worshiping God. She was perhaps thirty-five years old, and she was loving Jesus. Her face glowed as if it reflected a thousand-watt light bulb. Tears were flowing down her cheeks, and I heard her say, "I love You, Jesus."

As I watched her, it seemed to me that her face got brighter and brighter. I couldn't hear everything she was saying from where I was, and I was curious. So I walked down off the platform and stood in front of her. She ignored me. I leaned over and said, "You and the Lord are having a good time, aren't you, honey?" Still she didn't pay attention to me. I was insulted. I thought, *Doesn't she know I am the guest evangelist?*

I heard her say, "You are the Lily of the Valley. I love You. You are the Bright and Morning Star." I recognized that she was quoting love phrases from the Song of Solomon. She continued, "Thank You for being my husband, my friend." Somewhat awed, I turned and went back to the platform to sit down.

But I could not take my eyes off her. I knew she was experiencing the presence of God in a way that I never had. I watched her awhile, then walked back down to stand by her. She was still lost in worship, though I did not understand that then. She did not know I was there. So I returned to the platform a second time. Still watching her, I thought, *Maybe she doesn't hear well.*

So I walked down a third time and stood behind her so I could speak directly into her ear. Again I said to her, "You and the Lord are having a good time together, aren't you?" What I really wanted to say was, "What is going on? I don't understand what it is you are enjoying." I thought she could explain it to me, but still she did not acknowledge my presence.

This time when I returned to the platform I felt someone punch me. I recognized that it was the Lord trying to get my attention. He spoke to me so sweetly, "Fuchsia, you can have that if you want it." I didn't even know what *that* was, but I assumed He was referring to my fascination with the young worshiper.

I went to my room after the service and got on my knees. I said to the Lord, "All right, what is it? You said I could have the thing that made that girl so 'lost' she didn't know I was there. What is that?"

The Lord answered, "I seek a people who worship Me in spirit and truth."

I asked, "Is that worship? Then what have I been doing all these years?"

He was so kind. He didn't scold me. "Without this revelation of worship," He replied gently, "you have simply been having religious services."

"How can I have that?" I cried out. "Teach me to worship."

REVELATION OF WORSHIP

Then the Lord asked me three simple questions. First He inquired, "What would you do if you had just heard the gates of heaven click behind your heels, and you knew you were through with the devil forever?"

I responded vehemently, "You know I hate him!" I had spent months in a hospital as a patient, and I had followed behind casket after casket of family members who were being buried. I continued, "I would shout, 'Glory!'"

He said, "Shout it." And I did.

I told Him that I would cry, "Hallelujah!"

He said, "Do it." And I did.

Then He asked me what I would do if I looked up and saw Jesus for the first time.

I said that I would bow at His feet, kiss His nail-scarred hands and wash His feet with my tears.

He said, "Do it."

I meditated on the efficacious, vicarious, substitutionary and mediatorial work of Calvary, and suddenly I experienced a fresh glimpse of the Lamb of God. I began to bow before the Lamb who was slain, but He asked me to look up into His face. "When you see Me face to face," He asked, "what will you tell Me?"

When I heard those words, it was as if a dam within my soul broke, allowing torrents of praise to flood my lips. I told Him how wonderful He was. I recited the attributes of God I had learned in Bible college. I thanked Him for His omnipotence, omniscience and omnipresence, and I declared Him to be immutable, immaculate, emancipated, incarnate and divine. When I finished, He asked me if these were the only adjectives I had for Him.

With a sense of awe I responded simply, "You are wonderful."

A picture came to my mind, and I saw the face of Jesus before me as if it were framed. Then the frame faded. As I looked into His face, I told Him how much I loved Him. I had never done that in my life. I told Him how precious He was to me. I went on and on, trying to express my love for Him with my limited vocabulary.

When I was answering His three questions, it seemed as if just a few moments had passed. But it had actually been an hour and a half since I first knelt there. For the first time in my life I had been in the presence of God in such a way that I had lost all consciousness of time. I had begun to experience true worship—my heart responding to the love of God and expressing adoration and love to Him. All my years of Bible training, study and ministry had not evoked the response of worship from my heart that a few moments of divine revelation in His presence had.

As a sincere Methodist professor and pastor, I had considered myself to be a serious student of the Word who desired to rightly divide the word of truth. It was important to me to conduct church services in an orderly manner. I thought I understood what worship of an omnipotent God involved, and I regarded our worship services as important expressions of true reverence for God—the creature worshiping his Creator. Though we did honor God sincerely from our hearts, I now understand that we had defined worship very narrowly according to the tradition of our church fathers.

My renewed study of the Scriptures concerning worship, as well as my association with worshiping people, has helped me understand the divine destiny each of us has to become worshipers. Much of what is written in these pages is what I have learned as I have allowed my Teacher, the blessed Holy Spirit, to open my spiritual eyes to the purpose of God for our personal fulfillment—to become worshipers of God in spirit and in truth.

When I searched the Scriptures with this purpose in mind, many passages I had read before and thought I understood doctrinally began to live in my heart in a new way. Since that pivotal worship experience in my room, I have enjoyed God's manifest presence in praise and worship many times. I have also experienced the glory of His presence while studying His precious Word, observing communion and fellowshiping with other believers. Worshiping God has many facets of reality, as we shall discuss, that make it a central theme of the Scriptures. Understanding true spiritual worship is imperative for all believers who sincerely want to know God more intimately.

WORSHIP DEFINED

As we look at different aspects of worship in these chapters, our definition of worship will become more comprehensive. But we can begin with a simple working definition from Webster's Dictionary: "showing honor or reverence to a divine being or supernatural power; to regard with great, even extravagant respect, honor or devotion; to take part in an act of worship." The Old English spelling of the word is *worthship*, which aptly conveys the idea that the one to whom we show honor has worth. Worship is not an arrogant demand of God toward His creatures; it is rather the natural response from grateful hearts that comprehend the infinite "worthship" of God.

In our culture today there is such disrespect for government, leaders, clergy, laws, parental authority and even for life itself that we may find it difficult to understand the significance of the terms *honor* and *devotion,* even on a human level. The Scriptures describe the generation of people who will live in these last days:

> For men shall be lovers of their own selves, covetous, boasters, proud, blasphemers, disobedient to parents, unthankful, unholy, without natural affection, trucebreakers, false accusers, incontinent, fierce, despisers of those that are good, traitors, heady, highminded, lovers of pleasures more than lovers of God; having a form of godliness but denying the power thereof.
> —2 TIMOTHY 3:2–5

Worship is not a part of the wicked hearts Paul describes, even though they display some "form of godliness." Believers are commanded to turn away from such ungodly people (v. 5). Yet how many Christians are unwittingly influenced by their attitudes through the media or by a secret personal love of the world? Most of us can probably relate to (and repent for) at least one characteristic in the ominous list above.

But as we learn to enjoy a relationship with God out of a thankful heart that praises Him, reverence for God begins to displace worldly attitudes and to deter us from ungodly pursuits. Our proud hearts are humbled, and we experience true gratitude for God's goodness to us, which is so undeserved. Then we respond to His goodness in worship.

The biblical pattern of worship is based on the

surrender of the heart to the lordship of Christ. Without the heart reality of obedience and submission to the Word of God, we will never experience true worship in spirit and truth. Participation in the sacraments as well as in charismatic expressions of worship must reflect a heart that is bowed in gratitude and love for God in order to become true expressions of worship.

Clark Pinnock, in his theology of the Holy Spirit, defines worship in spirit and truth simply as worship that is grounded in the truth of Jesus and open to the Spirit, who takes us more deeply into it (John 4:24–25).[1]

Yielding to the Spirit of God by continually surrendering areas of our life to the lordship of Christ helps us to experience worship in spirit and truth.

A SURRENDERED HEART

Many Christians are talking about a renewed desire— even a new desire—to worship the Lord in a deeper, more meaningful way. But what is true worship? What is the absolute essence, the common denominator, for all expressions of worship?

According to the scriptural pattern, this is the fundamental essence of worship: I bow my heart before God Almighty and acknowledge His supreme lordship over my life. The divine essence of worship is realized through total surrender of the worshiper to the One worshiped. Only as we choose to acknowledge God in all our ways (Prov. 3:6) and give Him control of our lives and destinies can we become true worshipers of God.

Regardless of whatever negative circumstances, emotional pain or personal loss we may be facing, when everything that surrounds our lives screams, "God is unjust! He doesn't love me! He has forsaken me," we experience true worship when we can bow our hearts and respond, "The Lord is God. Blessed be the name of the Lord." Oswald Chambers confirms the attitude of the worshiper when he writes, "The spiritual order of Jesus Christ in my life is that I take what God has given me and give it back to Him; that is the essence of worship."[2]

The Old Testament patriarch Abraham is one of the most dramatic examples of the surrendered heart of a true worshiper. What was Abraham's response when God asked him to sacrifice his son of promise, Isaac, on the mountain? He rose up early and took the lad with him for the three-day journey. As he arrived at the place of sacrifice, he told those who were with him, "I and the lad will go yonder and worship, and come again to you" (Gen. 22:5).

The son of promise Abraham had waited so many years to receive was to be slain by his own hand at the command of God. Everything in a father's heart would naturally react violently to such a command. Yet Abraham had learned to love and trust the God who had led him out of his homeland, cut covenant with him and spoken to him many times. This God, who had promised to give Abraham a son by his wife, Sarah, and had done so miraculously, could only be worshiped, even in the face of unspeakable pain and personal loss.

Imagine the triumph and exhilaration of Abraham,

a man in covenant relationship with God, when he heard the voice of the angel of the Lord reversing the command to slay his son Isaac and commending him for his fear of God. Abraham received not only his son back from death but also a new revelation of God Himself. (See Hebrews 11:19.) When he looked and beheld a ram caught in a thicket, the ram that God sent to be the sacrifice instead of his son, he called the place *Jehovah-Jireh,* "the Lord will provide." The place of obedient surrender of all we hold dear to the One we worship will bring a fresh revelation of Himself to us that will satisfy our hearts and continually reveal our eternal destiny.

How did Job respond when he received word from messengers that all his livestock, his servants, his sons and his daughters had perished in a single day? Though his wife told him to curse God and die, the Scriptures reveal he had a worshiping heart: "Job arose, and rent his mantle, and shaved his head, and fell down upon the ground, and worshipped, and said, Naked came I out of my mother's womb, and naked shall I return thither: the LORD gave, and the LORD hath taken away; blessed be the name of the LORD" (Job 1:20–21). The Scriptures testify of Job's righteousness and declare that he did not sin in all his trial (Job 1:22; 2:3).

Job affirmed his faith in God when he declared, "Though he slay me, yet will I trust in him" (13:15). Only a trusting heart can worship God when it is filled with pain to the point of breaking. When we feel overwhelmed and don't know why God has allowed a painful situation to come into our lives, we must reaffirm our basic faith in God through our worshipful surrender to His lordship.

Though Job's friends falsely accused him and laid their judgments on him, Job was nevertheless vindicated before God. He received a new revelation of God as a result of the tragedies he suffered and was able to declare: "I have heard of thee by the hearing of the ear: but now mine eye seeth thee. Wherefore I abhor myself, and repent in dust and ashes" (Job 42:5–6). His fresh revelation of God made Job abhor himself because of the contrast he saw between humanity and deity.

God responded by commending Job and rebuking his friends, saying, "My wrath is kindled against thee [Eliphaz], and against thy two friends: for ye have not spoken of me the thing that is right, as my servant Job hath" (Job 42:7). Then, after Job prayed for his friends, God restored Job's fortunes and blessed his latter end more than his beginning. This worshiper triumphed through great tragedy by maintaining his surrender to the sovereignty of God.

The psalmist declared, "Deep calleth unto deep at the noise of thy waterspouts" (Ps. 42:7). When everything seems to crash down on us like a roaring waterfall, we look deep within our hearts and call out to the depths of God's heart to anchor our faith in God. Worship is the deep within us calling out to the deep in God. It is that expression of surrender from the depths of our souls that affirms our trust in God regardless of the pain or circumstances of our lives.

The apostle Paul admonished New Testament Christians to "present your bodies a living sacrifice, holy, acceptable unto God, which is your reasonable service" (Rom. 12:1). He understood that a surrendered life is the highest act of worship. As we consecrate our lives to God, they become a living sacrifice placed on the altar of surrender. Far from being extreme, a calling for just a few, the Bible calls this total surrender to God our "reasonable service."

A SILENT HEART

Our deepest worship may be expressed at times in a silent cry. Worship will not always constitute the forming of words or phrases to utter before God. But it will always involve the humble prostration of our souls before God as we revere His greatness in silence and stillness. The psalmist understood this when he wrote of the Lord, "Be still, and know that I am God" (Ps. 46:10).

Even in human love, affection is not always expressed verbally. Sometimes more is said through eye contact than could ever be expressed in words. Worship involves "eye contact" with God; it is staring at God! A worshiping heart longs to gaze upon the Beloved and know the fulfillment that comes when that gaze is returned.

AN AVAILABLE HEART

A worshiping heart understands that the time for worship is always the present. Worship cannot be postponed to a more convenient time, a time when life has become easier again. It does not matter that we have worshiped in the past, even if it was just yesterday.

Worshipers cannot be satisfied with worship in the past. Neither can they wait for the day when they will worship around the throne of God. They understand what Jesus meant when He said, "But the hour cometh, and now is, when the true worshippers shall worship the Father in spirit and in truth: for the Father seeketh such to worship him" (John 4:23). Worship is always in the present tense.

The psalmist declared, "Blessed is the people that know the joyful sound: they shall walk, O LORD, in the light of thy countenance. In thy name shall they rejoice all the day: and in thy righteousness shall they be exalted" (Ps. 89:15–16). True worshipers have heard the joyful sound, and they live in the presence of God and walk in His light. Learning to be continually available to Christ brings new dimensions of worship and revelation of God. No wonder they are blessed!

A LEARNING HEART

Just as in human relationships we learn to express our love to one another, so in worship we must learn to express our love to God. Worship is not a special gifting given to a select group of people, nor is it a talent with which we are born. Worship is the art of learning to express our love for God. We should not be impatient with ourselves if we are not able to worship as we would like. Learning the fullness of worship is a lengthy process and does not come easily. The lessons God brings into our lives to teach us about worship can sometimes be as dramatic as those of Abraham, Job and David.

Responding positively in difficult circumstances by choosing to worship rather than bemoaning our state will cause us to grow as worshipers. God delights in His children who desire to be worshipers. Jesus said He looks for them (John 4:23). Nothing pleases Him more than the quality of life displayed by a worshiper—one who honors God in great difficulties rather than complaining.

A REPENTANT HEART

Brokenness over our own sin characterizes a worshiping heart. When Mary came into the Pharisee's house to express her love for Jesus, she wept, washed His feet with her tears and anointed them with a costly ointment. The Pharisee condemned her as a sinner and accused Jesus for not knowing what kind of woman she was. But Jesus rebuked the Pharisee for not offering to wash His feet, the customary thing for a host to do. Then He declared this sinful woman forgiven of all her sins. (See Luke 7:36–50.)

Mary's tears were an outward manifestation of a heart that was deeply stirred before her Lord. She was repentant and so overcome with desire to express her love that she rejected the protocol of the day and barged into a private home uninvited. This was not a show. Her tears and her kisses were a sincere expression of her penitent heart.

AN EXPRESSIVE HEART

Mary's kisses are also characteristic of worship. One of the Greek words for worship—*proskuneo*—means "to kiss the hand toward; to do reverence or homage by kissing the hand; to bow one's self in adoration." Though men condemned Mary for her expression of worship, Jesus did not. He accepted her worship and forgave her sins. He looked at her heart and released her from the restraints of a pagan culture. What a beautiful assurance it is for us to know that when we worship, God will respond to us. He will speak to us, for He is eager to do so. Even though people may misunderstand and criticize our worship, God will satisfy the cries of our hearts.

King David's expressiveness when he escorted the ark of the covenant to Zion embarrassed his wife Michal. He danced in the streets in a linen ephod like a common man. She despised him because he had laid aside his kingdom robes, and she accused him of being a shameless man before the people. Because of Michal's criticism of her husband, a true worshiper, she was stricken with barrenness all the rest of her days. (See 2 Samuel 6:16–23.) We need to be very cautious about leveling criticism at God's people who are learning to worship. Even if their expressions seem strange or distasteful to us, God is looking at their hearts and accepting them on the basis of the sincerity of their worship.

A MATURE HEART

As we grow in our relationship with God, we will grow in our desire and our ability to worship. Spiritual maturity does not exempt one from being a worshiper; it enables one to worship more perfectly and to teach others to worship. When John the Revelator looked into heaven, he saw the twenty-four elders falling down before the Lamb with "harps, and golden vials full of odours," the prayers of saints, in worship before the throne (Rev. 5:8–9). We never outgrow our need to worship. Indeed, greater responsibility falls on the more mature to relate to God in worship and help others to do so.

We were made for worship. God created us with a longing to be rightly related to Him in a loving relationship that evokes worship. Without cultivating a worshiping heart that is cleansed from sin, surrendered to God and filled with adoration for our Lord, we will never know the fulfillment God intended for us to know. Surrender to His lordship in every area of our lives releases us into greater dimensions of worship that bring new revelation of God to our hearts. With each new revelation, we become more satisfied and walk more fully into the divine destiny for which we were created. The priority of worship God purposed will become the dynamic of our lives that brings true fulfillment.

The Imperative of Worship

The Object of Our Worship

BECAUSE MY CHURCH TRADITION DID NOT FOLLOW A biblical pattern for worship, when I was confronted with musical instruments such as drums and other percussion sounds in the sanctuary, I told God I didn't believe in them. He responded, "I do." Then He instructed me to read Psalms 149 and 150, which are filled with commands to praise God in loud and seemingly boisterous ways:

> Praise him for his mighty acts: praise him according to his excellent greatness. Praise him with the sound of the trumpet: praise him with the psaltery and harp. Praise him with the

timbrel and dance: praise him with stringed instruments and organs. Praise him upon the loud cymbals: praise him upon the high sounding cymbals. Let every thing that hath breath praise the LORD. Praise ye the LORD.

—PSALM 150:2–6

Learning to worship the infinite God is not an option for a Christian. The Scriptures set forth the worship of God as an imperative command. Both the Old and the New Testaments are filled with exhortations to praise and worship God for His goodness as well as for His mighty acts. This imperative for worship is not given, however, to make us recognize our subservience to an all-powerful God. It is not a decree from an egocentric Creator who desires to rule His creation.

God desires relationship with mankind. And God is love. So to know God is to love Him. And to love Him is to respond to His goodness, His greatness, His lovingkindness and all that He is with a heart filled with spontaneous praise and worship. To praise God is a command of the Scriptures that, when obeyed, will bring us into the presence of God. The psalmist instructed us to "enter into his gates with thanksgiving, and into his courts with praise" (Ps. 100:4).

When we praise God for what He *does,* we begin to experience His manifest presence, and our hearts then respond in worship, pouring out love and adoration for who He *is.* When we experience His "felt" presence, He satisfies our hearts and reveals Himself to us, many times unfolding another aspect of our personal destiny. Every believer who desires to find fulfillment in

God needs to understand the imperative for worship. The relationship of divine love we experience in our worship brings the deepest satisfaction to a human heart that it is capable of experiencing.

To consider whom we worship may at first seem to be proposing the obvious. However, since worship is fundamentally man's spirit responding to God's Spirit, man's concept of God will necessarily affect his response to God in worship. No one can experience worship to any greater degree than his concept of God allows. If we believe that God is an austere, harsh, severe, punitive being, we will worship Him out of fear and dread. If we see Him as a distant, uncaring Creator who is not interested in our daily lives, we will not cultivate an intimate relationship with Him through worship.

We would not think of sharing our true feelings, fears and desires with a God who maintains an aloofness from our intensely human desires and mundane tasks. And if our concept of God is limited to the understanding that He exists to meet our physical or financial needs, our praise will be limited to thanking Him only for meeting those needs. Our understanding of who God is must continually be enlarging in order for our praise and worship to reach higher realms of heavenly satisfaction. The Scriptures are filled with the self-revelation of God, who wants us to know Him as He is.

WHO GOD IS: THE NAMES OF GOD

The names of God reveal the character of God to us.

The progressive revelation of God to His people throughout biblical times always involved a revelation of a name that described an eternal aspect of His divine nature. For example, God revealed Himself to Moses at the burning bush as "I AM" (Exod. 3:14). The Hebrew word for "I AM" (*hayah*) denotes not only the existence of God, but also His abiding and remaining presence along with His accompanying presence. To people who had been born into a life of slavery for generations, this revelation of a God who not only existed but who would abide with them and accompany them must have been startling.

As New Testament Christians, we also need this revelation of the "I AM" presence of God. According to the Scriptures, we have to accept this fundamental revelation of God before we can come to Him. The writer to the Hebrews declared, "He that cometh to God must believe that he is, and that he is a rewarder of them that diligently seek him" (Heb. 11:6). As we dwell on the wonder of God, who was and is and forever shall be, our hearts will inevitably bow in worship to Him.

Jehovah (Yahweh) is another Old Testament title for God that He revealed first to Moses. It refers to the one true God who exists and who desires to manifest Himself continually in a greater way.[1]

God told Moses that He had appeared unto Abraham, Isaac and Jacob, but they did not know Him as Jehovah. (See Exodus 6:3.) So awesome was this revelation of God that the Jewish scribes substituted another word for Jehovah when they copied the Scriptures, out of reverence for who Jehovah is.[2]

The Old Testament records many names of God that

were compounds of the word *Jehovah* and a word that described an attribute of His character:

Jehovah-Jireh: The Lord Our Provider
Jehovah-Raphah: The Lord Our Healer
Jehovah-Nissi: The Lord Our Banner
Jehovah-Shalom: The Lord Our Peace
Jehovah-Ra-ah: The Lord My Shepherd
Jehovah-Tsidkenu: The Lord Our Righteousness
Jehovah-Shammah: The Lord Is Present

God wants to be everything to us that our human existence needs for comfort, health, prosperity, peace and righteousness. Even before the coming of Christ, God was communicating His loving attributes to His people by revealing His names and their significance. The attributes as well as the names of God, as revealed in Scripture, give us understanding of who God is.

WHO GOD IS: THE ATTRIBUTES OF GOD

Omnipresent. The Scriptures teach that God is omnipresent—everywhere present at all times. The psalmist asked the rhetorical question: "Whither shall I go from thy spirit? or whither shall I flee from thy presence?" (Ps. 139:7). Then he answered the question himself, declaring that God is in heaven, in hell and in the uttermost parts of the sea. He realizes there is no escaping God's presence, for even the darkness does not hide anything from Him.

The prophet Jeremiah records, "Am I a God at hand, saith the LORD, and not a God afar off? Can any hide himself in secret places that I shall not see him? .saith the LORD. Do not I fill heaven and earth? saith the LORD" (Jer. 23:23–24). And King Solomon, the wisest man who ever lived, wrote, "The eyes of the LORD are in every place, beholding the evil and the good" (Prov. 15:3). Although the word *omnipresence* is not a biblical word, this divine attribute is clearly taught in the Scriptures. Bible scholars agree:

> The Bible, which in regard to omnipresence, as in regard to the other transcendent attributes, clothes the truth of revelation in popular language, and speaks of exemption from the limitations of space in terms and figures derived from space itself. Thus, the very term "omnipresence" in its two component parts, "everywhere" and "present," contains a double inadequacy of expression, both the notion of "everywhere" and that of "presence" being spatial concepts. Although the Bible sometimes speaks of God's omnipresence with reference to the pervasive immanence of His being, it frequently contents itself with affirming the universal extent of God's power and knowledge.[3]

Omniscient. The omniscience—all knowledge—of God is another divine attribute that belongs only to Him. Again, the Bible scholars declare that God's omniscience extends to all spheres, to "all that is possible or actual."

> It extends to God's own being, as well as to what exists outside of Him in the created world. God

has perfect possession in consciousness of His own being. The unconscious finds no place in Him (Acts 15:18; 1 John 1:5). Next to Himself God knows the world in its totality. This knowledge extends to small as well as to great affairs (Matt 6:8, 32; 10:30); to the hidden heart and mind of man as well as to that which is open and manifest (Job 11:11; 34:21, 23; Ps. 14:2; 33:13–18; Prov. 5:21; Luke 16:15; Heb. 4:13; Rev. 2:23). It extends to all the divisions of time, the past, present and future alike (Job 14:17; Ps. 56:8; Isa. 41:22–24; 44:6–8; Jer. 1:5; Hos. 13:12; Mal. 3:16). It embraces that which is contingent from the human viewpoint as well as that which is certain (1 Sam. 23:9–12; Matt. 11:22–23).[4]

It is comforting to know that God is not only conscious of, but also cares divinely about, every detail of our lives. The psalmist wrote that God understands our thoughts and knows every word we utter. Then he exclaimed, "Such knowledge is too wonderful for me; it is high, I cannot attain unto it" (Ps. 139:6). Jesus comforted His disciples by instructing them concerning the caring omniscience of God:

> Are not two sparrows sold for a farthing? And one of them shall not fall on the ground without your Father. But the very hairs of your head are all numbered. Fear ye not therefore, ye are of more value than many sparrows.
> —MATTHEW 10:29–31

Omnipotent. The omnipotence—all power—of God

is perhaps His most misunderstood attribute. Unbelievers who have heard that God is all-powerful accuse Him for not using His power to keep bad things from happening, for not stopping wars or healing all diseases. In the darkness of their minds, they think that an all-powerful God who is good would put an end to all evil. They have not understood that God *chose* to allow His power to be limited by the power of choice He gave to mankind.

Though a day is coming when God will indeed put an end to all evil, in His great mercy He is allowing men to choose their destinies—to choose to be a part of His kingdom or the kingdom of Satan. God has provided a remedy for the destructive power of evil in the lives of all who will accept the sacrifice of Jesus' blood for the forgiveness of sin, that sin into which we were all born because of the disobedience of Adam and Eve.

If we choose to be a part of the kingdom of God, we will experience His omnipotent power on our behalf to redeem us from the curse of evil. But He will never use His power to coerce or force us to serve Him. That is the devil's way—to seduce and deceive men and women into serving him. God wants us to choose to serve Him because we love Him. So He limits His omnipotence to the power of choice He gave to mankind.

Bible scholars understand that this attribute of God was not fully revealed during Old Testament times:

> The formal conception of omnipotence as worked out in theology does not occur in the Old Testament. The substance of the idea is conveyed in various indirect ways.... A divine name

which signalizes this attribute is *Yahweh tseb-ha'oth*, Yahweh of Hosts. This name, characteristic of the prophetic period, describes God as the King surrounded and followed by the angelic hosts, and since the might of an oriental king is measured by the splendor of his retinue, as of great, incomparable power, the King Omnipotent (Ps. 24:10; Isa. 2:12).[5]

God was revealing Himself as the omnipotent God through the revelation of His names and by speaking through His prophets. Isaiah declared on God's behalf, "Yea, before the day was I am he; and there is none that can deliver out of my hand: I will work, and who shall let it?" (Isa. 43:13). And Jeremiah prayed, saying, "Ah Lord GOD! behold, thou hast made the heaven and the earth by thy great power and stretched out arm, and there is nothing too hard for thee" (Jer. 32:17).

In the New Testament we read Jesus' words: "With men this is impossible; but with God all things are possible" (Matt. 19:26). It is a wonderful security to know that we serve an all-powerful, all-knowing God of love. Our temporal and eternal safety lies in the strength of our relationship with Him.

Eternal. The eternal nature of God is an attribute that should be mentioned, though our natural minds cannot fathom that which transcends our framework of time. That God has always existed and always will exist and that we can live eternally—forever—with Him is a mystifying concept to our finite human intellect. Though the word *eternal* in both the Hebrew and the Greek languages does refer to continuous existence, unlimited time and unending future, it also denotes a quality of life. Bible scholars underscore this fact of the eternal quality of divine life available to man:

> Our Lord decisively set the element of time in abeyance, and took His stand upon the fact and quality of life—life endless by its own nature. Of that eternal life He is Himself the guarantee— "Because I live, ye shall live also" (John 14:19). Therefore said Augustine, "Join thyself to the eternal God, and thou wilt be eternal."[6]

The prayer Jesus prayed just before His death revealed His desire that everyone who believes in Him enjoy this quality of eternal life as He described it:

> Father, the hour is come; glorify thy Son, that thy Son also may glorify thee: As thou hast given him power over all flesh, that he should give eternal life to as many as thou hast given him. And this is life eternal, that they might know thee the only true God, and Jesus Christ, whom thou hast sent.
> —JOHN 17:1–3

According to the Scriptures, having eternal life means to know God and His Son Jesus Christ. Have we understood that to know Christ as our Savior means we are partakers now, in the present, of the divine quality of eternal life that makes God who He is? Though much of our earthly lives are limited by the responsibilities and duties of time schedules, we can enjoy the reality of eternity as we cultivate a relationship with an eternal God.

Many of our frustrations of trying to manage our affairs in "time" will be resolved as we learn to prioritize our lives around what is important in the light of eternal values. The workaholic and the couch potato alike will learn to use time differently when their priorities change in the light of eternity. Jesus died to give us a quality of life—eternal life. He declared that He came to give us life—more abundantly (John 10:10). While that does not negate the fact of living forever with Him, it does give us hope that we can enjoy a relationship in the present that goes beyond our temporal circumstances.

We have discussed only briefly a few of the attributes of God to help us understand this wonderful Creator and Savior who desires relationship with mankind. He has revealed Himself in the Scriptures and throughout history as a God of love, whose promise of abundant and eternal life is for all who will choose to know Him and serve Him. Worship is an automatic response of the heart that learns truly to know this loving God.

THE NATURE OF GOD

It can be argued that the attributes of God are a part of the nature of God and that the two cannot be separated from each other. However, simply for the sake of discussion, we will consider the essence of the nature of God here apart from His attributes, without meaning to separate them in the overall picture of who God is. Considering the nature of God, as well as His names and attributes, serves to inspire our worship of Him. To know God is to love Him; to love Him is to worship Him.

Love. The Scriptures teach that the nature of God is love: "God is love; and he that dwelleth in love dwelleth in God, and God in him" (1 John 4:16). One of my greatest discoveries about God was that because He is love, He has a need. I was trained in a theology that taught that God is all-sufficient, having need of nothing. But that cannot be completely true because God is love. It is the nature of love to need someone to receive that love. Therefore, as we mentioned earlier, God has a need to love and be loved. Though there is infinite communion and love between the members of the Trinity—God the Father, God the Son and God the Holy Spirit—creation is evidence that God desired to have a family into which He could pour His love.

I wrote in my book *God's Dream* concerning this love-nature of God:

> Though our theological understanding of God's self-existence, which pictures God as having need of nothing, often prevails in our thinking, all Scripture testifies to the contrary, showing us that God had a need. God is love (1 John 4:8). Love is not merely an attribute of God's character, but the essence of His Being. The nature of love requires a recipient, one who will respond by choice to the love given. Because God is love, He needed someone to respond to His love. Because of that longing, They said among Themselves, "Let us make man in our image" (Gen. 1:26). God expressed His need in His desire for a family, one into whom He could pour His very nature. His purpose in creating

mankind was to have someone with whom to
fellowship and share His love.[7]

The extravagant love of God motivates everything
He has ever done, including the creation of our world
and of mankind. It is the devil who has so maligned
the wonderful nature of God and caused such chaos
for all of humanity. Life apart from God, regardless of
outward circumstances, is a kind of hell—a separation
from all that is loving and good. Only God can define
love for His creatures, who so long to love and be
loved. As we come into relationship with God,
receiving even the tiniest glimpse of His love is so
intoxicating that our spontaneous response is to worship Him.

Holiness. God is holy just as He is love. Neither
aspect of His nature can exist apart from the other.
Without holiness, there is no love. And without love,
there is no holiness. When God commanded that we be
holy even as He is holy (1 Pet. 1:16), He did not mean
to frustrate us by asking us to make ourselves holy,
which of course is impossible. Rather, He was
describing who we would become as we partake of His
holiness. The more we behold Him in worship, the
more we will reflect His holiness in our lives. We will
be less likely to define holiness according to church tradition or our legal interpretation of the Scriptures.

The apostle Paul declared, "But we all, with open
face beholding as in a glass the glory of the Lord, are
changed into the same image from glory to glory, even
as by the Spirit of the Lord" (2 Cor. 3:18). The image of
God reflects His love and His holiness as the essence of

His nature. According to this scripture, as we behold Him in worship, our nature will be changed to reflect the nature of God.

As the Holy Spirit reveals Jesus to us, He releases His divine, life-giving power within us, enabling us to exchange our unholiness for the true holiness of God. To the degree that we are willing to give up our way, our will, our wants, our walk, our words, our work and our warfare, we can partake of the nature of God and experience His holiness in our lives. That is what it means to take up our cross and follow Christ, to die daily, so that we can enjoy the resurrection power of Jesus manifested through our lives.

The prophet Isaiah had an awesome encounter with the holiness of God when He saw into heaven and beheld angelic beings surrounding the throne of God crying, "Holy, holy, holy" (Isa. 6:3). When he beheld the holiness of God, Isaiah became painfully aware of his personal unholiness, the uncleanness of his own flesh, and he cried out, "Woe is me! for I am undone; because I am a man of unclean lips…for mine eyes have seen the King, the LORD of hosts" (Isa. 6:5).

However painful this self-revelation may have been, it resulted in Isaiah's cleansing and equipping for greater service for the Lord. To become holy is to see God's holiness and allow Him to reveal our need for repentance from our unholiness. Then as we are cleansed and receive the holiness of God for our lives, we can be equipped for increasing fruitfulness in building the kingdom of God on the earth. This process of revelation and cleansing will lead us into ever greater depths of worship as we continue to behold the nature of a holy God.

Though we cannot go further in our study of the nature of God in these pages, even this thumbnail sketch of God's love and holinesss can inspire our worship of Him. Such a loving heavenly Father is worthy of our love. He is worthy of our commitment to pursue Him the rest of our lives so that we may know Him and love Him with all our hearts. He is worthy!

THE TRIUNE GOD

Considering God as the triune being will help us to more fully understand who He is and deepen our worship of Him. To this end, but without presuming to separate the Trinity, let's look individually at the three persons of the Godhead—God the Father, God the Son and God the Holy Spirit. As I have mentioned, since the beginning of time God has desired to reveal Himself to mankind. I pointed out how each of His Old Testament names represents a divine revelation of another aspect of His Being unfolded to His beloved creation.

But perhaps the most significant revelation of God as Father is creation itself. As I explained earlier, God created mankind so that He could have a family. Because God is love, He needed someone to respond to His love by choice. God's purpose in creating mankind was to have someone with whom to fellowship and share His love. It cost the Godhead inestimable suffering to bring Their love to us. We cannot comprehend the suffering of God in eternity. Knowing that man would fail the love test by choosing to disobey Him rather than walking in relationship with Him and that Jesus would have to become the sacrificial Lamb to redeem us to Himself, God suffered that incalculable loss. Yet so great was the Father's need for someone into whom He could pour His love—a family—that He proceeded to fulfill His dream by creating mankind.

God's hurt-love produced the nature of the Lamb. His family would share His nature, the Lamb Spirit of hurt-love. In the types of the Old Testament, we see the suffering heavenly Father each time a man had to choose his own spotless lamb, tie it with a cord and take it to the temple to offer it as a sacrifice. The Father's heart is beating with a longing to impart to us the same quality of love the Godhead enjoyed in eternity. It is no wonder the highest order of worship found in the Book of Revelation is expressed in the cry, "Worthy is the Lamb that was slain to receive power, and riches, and wisdom, and strength, and honour, and glory, and blessing" (Rev. 5:12). God the Father knew from the beginning what it would cost to have a family, and in His great love, He proceeded with His wonderful plan that included Jesus becoming the spotless Lamb to redeem us from sin.[8]

God the Son

The writer to the Hebrews shows us another way in which the Father revealed Himself and communicated His love to His people:

> God, who at sundry times and in divers manners spake in time past unto the fathers by the

> prophets, hath in these last days spoken unto us
> by his Son, whom he hath appointed heir of all
> things, by whom also he made the worlds.
> —HEBREWS 1:1–2

Jesus Christ is the ultimate revelation of God the Father. During the last days of Jesus' life on earth, one of His disciples told Him that he would be satisfied if Jesus would show him the Father. Jesus' response to this question may surprise some today as it must have the disciples:

> Have I been so long time with you, and yet hast
> thou not known me, Philip? He that hath seen
> me hath seen the Father; and how sayest thou
> then, Shew us the Father? Believest thou not that
> I am in the Father, and the Father in me?
> —JOHN 14:9–10

Obviously, worship of the Father is worship of the Son. By worshiping God in spirit and truth, we worship the triune God. But as we deepen our appreciation and honor for God the Son revealed in the life of Jesus Christ, our desire to worship God will increase.

Jesus would not have allowed men to worship Him if He were not worthy to receive their worship. He would have said, as Peter did when Cornelius fell at his feet and worshiped, "Stand up; I myself also am a man" (Acts 10:26). In receiving men's worship when He walked the earth, Jesus was declaring Himself to be God—completely worthy of our worship.

Jesus' birth was marked by several instances of

worship by different people—the shepherds, Simeon, Anna, the wise men. During His earthly ministry He received worship from a leper (Matt. 8:2); a ruler (Matt. 9:18); and the Syrophoenician woman (Matt. 15:25). Christ's disciples worshiped Him after He calmed the storm (Matt. 14:33), and the two Marys did after His resurrection (Matt. 28:9). The elders and living creatures revealed in the Book of Revelation worship Him (Rev. 4:9–11). And the Scriptures declare that one day every living creature will worship Him:

> Wherefore God also hath highly exalted him, and given him a name which is above every name: that at the name of Jesus every knee should bow, of things in heaven, and things in earth, and things under the earth; and that every tongue should confess that Jesus Christ is Lord, to the glory of God the Father.
>
> —PHILIPPIANS 2:9–11

One of the most tender pictures of the Son of God, a picture that ought to evoke deep reverence and worship, even awe, in the heart of believers, is found in the Book of the Revelation. John the Revelator reveals to us what he saw:

> And I saw in the right hand of him that sat on the throne a book written within and on the backside, sealed with seven seals. And I saw a strong angel proclaiming with a loud voice, Who is worthy to open the book, and to loose the seals thereof? And no man in heaven, nor in earth, neither under the earth, was able to open the

book, neither to look thereon. And I wept much, because no man was found worthy to open and to read the book, neither to look thereon. And one of the elders saith unto me, Weep not: behold, the Lion of the tribe of Judah, the Root of David, hath prevailed to open the book, and to loose the seven seals thereof. And I beheld, and, lo, in the midst of the throne and of the four beasts, and in the midst of the elders, stood a Lamb as it had been slain, having seven horns and seven eyes, which are the seven Spirits of God sent forth into all the earth. And he came and took the book out of the right hand of him that sat upon the throne. And when he had taken the book, the four beasts and four and twenty elders fell down before the Lamb, having every one of them harps, and golden vials full of odours, which are the prayers of saints. And they sung a new song, saying, Thou art worthy to take the book, and to open the seals thereof: for thou wast slain, and hast redeemed us to God by thy blood out of every kindred, and tongue, and people, and nation.

—Revelation 5:1–9

Jesus—the Son of God, the Lamb who was slain— will receive worship and honor throughout eternity. As we behold Him, our hearts cannot help but bow with the elders in humble gratitude for His unfathomable sacrifice that redeemed us and brought us back into His wonderful presence. Bowing, prostrating ourselves, singing, praying—all are proper activities in worship, born of a heart responding to the love of God. As we meditate on these glimpses of eternity where worship is modeled for us, our hearts can be enlarged to worship God the Son in the manner of which He is deserving.

ᐁ GOD THE HOLY SPIRIT ᐅ

When Jesus promised His disciples that He would send the Holy Spirit to them, He described Him as the Comforter who would "reprove the world of sin, and of righteousness, and of judgment" (John 16:8). He called Him the "Spirit of truth" and said He would guide them into all truth, show them things to come and glorify Jesus. It is unfortunate that many Christians know so little about this Third Person of the Godhead. Some refer to Him as an "it." Others think of Him as an influence or power or even "tongues."

In my two-volume study of the Holy Spirit, I wrote:

> The Holy Spirit is the Third Person of the Godhead who came to bring us into right relationship with God. The Holy Spirit wants us to commune and fellowship with Him in an intimacy that is greater than any we would share with another person. Many of us do not enjoy this kind of relationship with the Holy Spirit because we do not think of Him as a Person. We could even have received the baptism of the Holy Spirit and still not recognize Him as a divine Personality. Before we can relate to the Holy Spirit properly, we must accept the truth that He

is, in fact, a Person. Being a person involves the power of intellect, the power of volition, or will, and the power of emotional response...The Holy Spirit simply has come to reveal Jesus, the lovely Savior, to all who will respond to His invitation to receive eternal life. The Spirit offers eternal life to all who will accept the sacrifice of Jesus' blood for their sins. Only the Holy Spirit has the power to save our souls and change us into the image of Christ.[9]

The Old Testament reveals the blessed Holy Spirit to us through types and symbols. One of the most beautiful types of the Holy Spirit is found in the holy anointing oil that was given to Moses. He is symbolized, among other things, as a gentle dove, as refreshing rain and as wind and fire. In the New Testament, Jesus clearly revealed to His disciples the Holy Spirit who was to come. Then, just before His ascension, He told the disciples to wait in the upper room until He sent the Holy Spirit to fill them with His power.

Communion with the Holy Spirit is one of seven moods of the Holy Spirit through which we can relate to Him. In my study of the Holy Spirit referenced above, I describe seven different moods in which the Holy Spirit expresses Himself: convicting, counseling, compassion, cleansing, commanding, conquering and communion.[10]

The Scriptures clearly distinguish these divine responses of the Holy Spirit to human need. It is our need for communion that brings us into multifaceted realms of prayer through the Spirit that include petition, thanksgiving, intercession, praise and—as we are discussing here—worship.

Too often we think of prayer as simply our talking to God. We don't realize that God the Father, God the Son and God the Holy Spirit want to talk back to us. True prayer is two-way communication with God. Though communion with God involves many kinds of prayer, when we look at communion in its deepest meaning we understand that it is the most intimate of all realms of prayer. It is that relationship ordained of God that will completely satisfy our hearts as well as His own.

Our relationship with God should be characterized by an ever-deepening experience of prayer that brings us into true communion with God. As we come to know Him in His unspeakable greatness and unfathomable goodness, our hearts are filled with a divine love and adoration for Him that can be expressed only in worship. From our discussion of the attributes and nature of God, we can conclude that *who* we worship has everything to do with *why* we worship. We can realize our true identity and divine destiny only as we cultivate a personal relationship with a loving, holy God who desires to have fellowship with us.

True Spiritual Worship

Key to a Dynamic Life

I MENTIONED EARLIER THAT BECAUSE GOD IS LOVE, HE wanted to have a family who would reciprocate His extravagant love. He desired to have children who would be like Him in order to pour His love into them and enjoy communion with them forever. When Adam and Eve failed to respond correctly to God's love through their disobedience to His command, they died to that divine relationship of love they enjoyed with their Creator—that communion, fellowship and friendship they knew when He talked with them in the garden. Their purpose for being was thwarted and forfeited by their wrong choice.

As we trace the hand of God throughout the Old

Testament, we see that every time God connects with man He is trying to restore a measure of the communion He had with Adam and Eve in the Garden. He cut covenant with Abraham, established the Passover, gave the elaborate Mosaic law involving sacrifices and offerings to the nation of Israel, inhabited the tabernacle of David and the temple of Solomon—all as part of the process of restoring mankind to the fellowship with our Creator that was lost because of that first couple's sin.

Not until God became man in Jesus Christ was the promise of complete restoration of man to his original destiny made a reality. Jesus, through His obedience to the Father and His death on the cross, made it possible for mankind to be restored to divine fellowship with God. The deepest longing in the heart of every person is still to know the destiny for which he was created. We can discover that divine destiny only to the measure that we are restored to our worship of God.

Through our acceptance of Jesus' perfect sacrifice when we are born again we are restored to the love relationship God had destined for mankind to enjoy. We understand that when we accept this sacrifice, our dead spirits are made alive unto God. We who were dead in trespasses and sins can once again begin to commune with God through worship and allow Him to pour His divine love into our hearts. (See Colossians 2:13.) Then we can begin to find answers to the five innate questions each of us has in his heart. Who made me? Who is God? What is the purpose of my life? How can I fulfill my destiny? After this life, what?[1]

As we cultivate our relationship with God, He

begins to reveal His eternal plan for our lives. Without that relationship, our dynamic for living is misguided, self-serving and altogether unsatisfactory.

We use the term "calling of God" in the church to describe our burdens to preach or teach, give our lives to missions or to children's work or follow other worthwhile pursuits that will help people come into the kingdom of God. We have been taught that as we fulfill the calling of God on our lives, we will find fulfillment and be successful in life. However, this definition of "calling" is too narrow to encompass the scriptural understanding of personal destiny that results in living a dynamic life.

Have you considered why the Lord called you to be a child of God? Was it to become a powerful preacher of the gospel, to be a missionary in a far-off country or to be a good husband and father or wife and mother? Is your calling to be a successful business person or an efficient administrator? While these may be valid pursuits in life in obedience to the calling of God, we need to look more closely into the Scriptures to identify our true calling.

In my study of the Scriptures, I have discovered at least forty-one calls that apply to the lives of believers. Consider, for example, that we are called out of darkness into His marvelous light. The appendix contains a list of these callings along with Scripture references.

But not one of these is our primary call. When God created Adam there were no churches to pastor, no heathen to preach the gospel to and no businesses or offices to manage. We have stated that the primary reason God created Adam was to fulfill God's desire for

a family with whom He could enjoy sweet communion. His first priority is the same today as then: to
enjoy His children in a love relationship. Jesus
declared, "If a man love me, he will keep my words:
and my Father will love him, and we will come unto
him, and make our abode with him" (John 14:23).

*Our primary calling is our destiny to enjoy relation-
ship with God, not to work for Him.* The work God gave
Adam to do was to have dominion over the earth. He
was in charge of taking care of the place where he
would live with his descendants and where God would
come to walk with him and commune with him. God's
desire for believers is to cultivate a love relationship
with each of us. In the context of that relationship He
will then give us specific tasks to do. Yet the tasks
should never diminish the priority of relationship with
Him.

Of course, God has ordained the church, the body of
Christ in the earth, to serve one another as we serve
God. But we must be careful to prioritize our calling
the way God does and not according to man's perspective. God intends that our service to the body of Christ
and to lost humanity proceed out of relationship with
Himself. That relationship of worship—the creature to
the Creator, the redeemed to the Redeemer—will
motivate us to serve out of a heart of love for God.

I am convinced that whatever God does to advance
His purpose on the earth is born out of a worshiping
people. When the woman at the well asked Jesus questions about worship, He responded, "The hour
cometh, and now is, when the true worshippers shall
worship the Father in spirit and in truth: for the Father

seeketh such to worship him" (John 4:23). It was the woman's question and Jesus' answer that led me to seek God and search the Scriptures in order to understand what Jesus meant by worship in "spirit and truth." God seeks worshipers who will cultivate a love relationship with Him. He values our relationship with Him more than anything we can or will ever do for Him.

SPIRITUAL BARRENNESS

Unfortunately, the church has often reversed this worship priority, placing greater value on service than on relationship with God. Because of this wrong emphasis on works, the church has suffered a history of barrenness and has been ineffective in its service. God declared through the prophet Zechariah that every nation who did not go to Jerusalem and worship the King would have no rain. The blessing of God would be withheld from the land of all who refused to go up and worship (Zech. 14:16–19). He confirmed the priority of God's heart to have relationship with His people based on their faithfulness to worship Him. His command for them to worship brought with it a conditional promise of blessing. Simply stated in the negative: No worship, no rain.

Job describes how God gives the blessing of rain by forming small drops of water from the vapors He draws up, which the clouds pour down as moisture so that abundant showers fall on mankind (Job 36:27–28). In much the same way, our worship ascends unto God as spiritual vapors that God receives as raw materials from which He can rain power and blessing on us and on the land in which we dwell. Without the presence of God to refresh our lives, we become like a barren wasteland.

A BIBLICAL TYPE OF TRUE SPIRITUAL WORSHIP

God commanded Moses to make a fragrant perfume to be used as part of the Israelites' worship expression. In Exodus 30:34, He gave Moses a detailed recipe for this perfume, which was not to be used for anything other than the purpose God specified. It remains for us today a beautiful Old Testament picture—or type—of true spiritual worship. The perfume was to be made from four fragrant spices: stacte, onycha, galbanum and pure frankincense of equal portions. These fragrant spices were to be ground to powder and placed in front of the testimony in the tent of meeting, the place where God would meet with His people. God was careful to give specific instructions concerning the worship that was acceptable to Him. Through the natural ingredients that made a sweet-smelling perfume in His presence, He was teaching us spiritual qualities that are sweet to Him.

Spontaneity

Stacte (Hebrew *nataph*, "drops" [Job 36:27]; *stakte*, meaning "oozing out in drops")[2] is a gum resin that oozes spontaneously from the stem and leaves of the plants that contain it. Spontaneity in worship springs from a grateful heart. True worship will be a spontaneous response from our hearts to the goodness of God. As we spend time in prayer and in reading the

Word of God each day, we will see how worthy God is of our worship. Our hearts will begin to "ooze" with gratitude for His lovingkindness that is better than life.

Honesty

Onycha (*shecheleth*; compare Arabic *suchalat,* "filings," "husks") is supposed to denote the operculum found in certain species of marine gastropod mollusks. The operculum is a disk attached to the upper side of the back part of the "foot" of the mollusk. When the animal draws itself into its shell, the operculum comes last and closes the mouth of the shell. The onycha emits a peculiar odor when burned, and it is still used in combination with other perfumes by the Arab women of Upper Egypt and Nubia.[3]

Onycha typifies first of all that real worship comes from a deep heart reality within us, just as the mollusk is found in the depths of the sea. God reproached His people on one occasion saying, "These people come near to me with their mouth and honor me with their lips, but their hearts are far from me. Their worship of me is made up only of rules taught by men" (Isa. 29:13, NIV). Worship that is taught by the rules of men is unauthorized incense going up to God. The sons of Aaron offered unauthorized incense on the altar, and God struck them dead with fire that came from His presence. We cannot pretend to worship or choose to worship in our own way without paying the consequences for our actions.

God's priority is a genuine heart response of love from His children. He knows whether we are truly expressing our hearts to Him or just going through motions we have learned or tradition we have been taught. The onycha's function to open and close the mouth of the mollusk is also a picture for us of the openness and honesty God desires in our worship. The apostle Paul declares, "But we all, with open face beholding as in a glass the glory of the Lord, are changed into the same image from glory to glory, even as by the Spirit of the Lord" (2 Cor. 3:18). And the writer to the Hebrews confirms:

> All things are naked and opened unto the eyes of him with whom we have to do. Seeing then that we have a great high priest, that is passed into the heavens, Jesus the Son of God, let us hold fast our profession.... Let us therefore come boldly unto the throne of grace, that we may obtain mercy, and find grace to help in time of need.
> —Hebrews 4:13–16

Openness results from trust and confidence in a love relationship in which we do not have to fear rejection or any negative response to who we are or what we are offering. One of the deepest cries of the human heart is to have the kind of relationship in which we can be open and vulnerable with our thoughts and feelings, fears and shortcomings, and know that we will be accepted and loved in spite of them. God offers us this wonderful security of being "accepted in the beloved" (Eph. 1:6).

The Scriptures admonish us to come boldly into the presence of God, where we will find the grace we need for every situation. A worshiping heart never needs to despair no matter what kind of pain or heartache it faces in life. We can open our hearts to Jesus, who offers us the rest for our souls that can be found only in His presence:

> Come unto me, all ye that labour and are heavy laden, and I will give you rest. Take my yoke upon you, and learn of me; for I am meek and lowly in heart: and ye shall find rest unto your souls. For my yoke is easy, and my burden is light.
> —MATTHEW 11:28–30

Brokenness

Galbanum (Hebrew *chelbenah; chalbdne*), a third ingredient in the perfume of worship, is a gum resin that occurs in small, round, semitranslucent tears or in brownish-yellow masses. It has a pleasant aromatic odor and a bitter taste, and is today imported from Persia.[4]

The semitranslucent tears and bitter taste represent a picture of the brokenness that God desires in our worship. The psalmist declared, "The sacrifices of God are a broken spirit; a broken and contrite heart, O God, you will not despise" (Ps. 51:17, NIV) and "The LORD is close to the brokenhearted and saves those who are crushed in spirit" (Ps. 34:18, NIV).

And Jesus taught, "Blessed are they that mourn: for they shall be comforted" (Matt. 5:4). As we acknowledge our need of a Savior and realize the depravity of our hearts without Him, the reality of Matthew 5:4 will break our hearts and bring a mourning to our spirits that will evoke worship. God asks that we come into His presence with an open-hearted spontaneity that reveals the depths of a broken and contrite heart. That is our responsibility for experiencing true spiritual worship.

Purity

The fourth ingredient in the perfume of worship is frankincense, which corresponds to God's involvement in our worship. The root meaning of frankincense (Hebrew *lebonah*) is whiteness, referring to the milky color of the fresh juice obtained from certain trees of the genus *Boswellia,* growing on the limestone rocks of south Arabia and Somaliland. Some of the trees grow to a considerable height and send down their roots to extraordinary depths. The gum is obtained by incising the bark.

Frankincense is often associated with myrrh (Song of Sol. 3:6; 4:6). It was used as an offering to the infant Savior (Matt 2:11). An especially "pure" kind, *lebonah zakkah,* was presented with the showbread (Lev 24:7). This pure white substance, obtained by breaking the branch of the tree, represents the holiness God alone can bring to our worship. The English word is derived from the Old French *franc encens,* that is, "pure incense."[5]

Purity is not a quality that we sinful creatures can contribute to the perfume of worship. Jesus Christ is the spotless Lamb of God whose body was broken to take away the sins of the world. The Scriptures declare, "God made him who had no sin to be sin for us, so that in him we might become the righteousness of God" (2

Cor. 5:21, NIV). It is incredible to think that when we approach God in worship, Jesus Himself worships with us. He is involved in our worship.

The Scriptures clearly teach this wonderful reality: "He [Jesus] says, 'I will declare your name to my brothers; in the presence of the congregation I will sing your praises'" (Heb. 2:12, NIV). The prophet Zephaniah also spoke of this reality when he declared, "The LORD thy God in the midst of thee is mighty; he will save, he will rejoice over thee with joy; he will rest in his love, he will joy over thee with singing" (Zeph. 3:17). The purity of God mingles with the sacrifices of our broken, contrite hearts to become a sweet-smelling fragrance before the throne of God as our worship ascends unto Him. No wonder we are changed from glory to glory into His image as we wait before Him in true spiritual worship.

Many Christians seem discontent and frustrated in life, suffering defeat and living without the joy Jesus promised us. They have not discovered the divine destiny that God ordained for them as worshipers. Perhaps part of their problem is a lack of true reverence toward God, which comes by revelation as we surrender completely to the lordship of Christ.

4

Reverence Toward God

An Attitude Expressed

REVERENCE FOR GOD IS NOT AN ENTIRELY FOREIGN concept to most people. We have heard the word *reverence* used, especially as it applies to our attitude toward God and our behavior in the sanctuary. It is proper to be reverent in God's house. But what is reverence? Is it simply an attitude of politeness that we express when we refer to God or attend church? Or is it something more? What should reverence look like in the life of a Christian? We need to have a clear understanding of what it means to be reverent if we are to walk in obedience to God's Word. The Scriptures instruct us to serve God acceptably with reverence and godly fear:

> Therefore, since we receive a kingdom which cannot be shaken, let us show gratitude, by which we may offer to God an acceptable service with reverence and awe; for our God is a consuming fire.
>
> —HEBREWS 12:28–29, NAS

Gratitude to God should be the motivating force by which we offer our acceptable service with reverence. In the New Testament, the Greek word *aidos* is translated as "reverence." It means "awe and godly fear." The heart of a worshiper, as we have discussed, is one that is truly grateful for the goodness of God to redeem, forgive, heal and restore our broken lives to intimate relationship with Him. Gratitude for "so great a salvation" evokes reverence—awe and godly fear—from sinful creatures who are being redeemed from their sin.

The human heart is naturally unthankful and unresponsive to a loving God. It requires a work of God in our hearts to enable us to offer acceptable worship. Matthew Henry, the popular Bible commentator, describes the supernatural grace necessary for worship:

> It is only the grace of God that enables us to worship God in a right manner: Nature cannot come up to it; it can produce neither that precious faith nor that holy fear that is necessary to acceptable worship.[1]

A REVERENT LIFE

True reverence for God involves living a reverent life,

52

not just acting reverent in church. Serving God with reverence means showing Him honor and respect in every area of our lives. We understand that God has come to earth in Christ and that Christ dwells in our hearts by the Holy Spirit. A genuine revelation of this reality changes our attitude toward all of life. We learn to revere the presence of God that lives *in* us whether we are sitting in a restaurant, doing the dishes, driving our car or engaging in casual conversation.

If Christ is truly King in our lives, reverence for Him will be seen in our submission to His lordship in the decisions that govern our daily lives. Reverence should so impact our lives that it shapes our talk and our walk in every relationship and endeavor. I do not believe that slang has a place in a Christian's vocabulary. Any euphemism for the name of God cheapens our respect for the One we worship. My life should reflect the glory of God in every word I speak. For the Holy Spirit to be comfortable living in me, I need to understand how to show reverence to Him at all times.

How do we show reverence? Is it by the way we sing? Pray? By our silence? Is it confined to some particular tradition or form of worship? If we are cultivating a grateful heart, we will exhibit a reverent attitude in every aspect of our lives. We will continually become more sensitive to irreverent speech and unkind attitudes that do not bring glory to God. What place do we give to the presence of God twenty-four hours a day? Do we shelve Him during work hours and times of recreation? We cannot ignore God's presence in our lives if we are living in reverence and fear of Him.

I was in the presence of a person one time who was

more aware of God than he was of the people around him. He was sitting in my office with a group of people as we discussed a serious problem. But he was connected to God in such a way that as we discussed the problem, I began to see the glory of God on his countenance. In a few moments, he spoke with a wisdom from above that gave a divine answer to the issue we were discussing. He had learned to cultivate the presence of God to such an extent that being with people did not interrupt his communion with Him.

The Scriptures teach us that "the fear of the LORD is the beginning of wisdom" (Prov. 9:10). This fear (Hebrew *yirah*) is not a cringing fear that has torment; that kind of fear comes from Satan. To fear God is to respect Him much as we would an earthly king. We are the children of the eternal King, and there is a protocol that must be practiced in the presence of a king. It is true that we have a loving relationship with God as our heavenly Father. But we must never allow familiarity to erode the reverence He is due as the omnipotent King under whose benevolent rule we will live for all eternity.

REVERENCE EXPRESSES LOVE

We need to understand that reverence and respect are expressions of love. To respect and revere God is to love Him. And to love Him is to obey Him. Reverence will characterize our love for God. Because I loved my daddy deeply—he was my dearest friend—I lived with a certain fear of displeasing him. When he made a rule for me, I did my best to keep it so that he would be pleased with me. Reverence for God will give us this kind of desire to keep His commandments in obedience to His Word. Reverence will cause us to respect His Word, His family, His house, the Sabbath and His tithe and to do all He has commanded us to do. He is God, and we must learn to reverence Him as God. The more we allow reverence to have its rightful place in our lives, the more obedient we will become to His will.

According to the Scriptures, our lives are temples for the presence of God. The apostle Paul wrote, "For we are the temple of the living God; just as God said, 'I will dwell in them and walk among them; and I will be their God, and they shall be My people'" (2 Cor. 6:16, NAS). God Himself wants to dwell in us in all of His holiness, power and love. He wants to express His love through us as we obey the Word of God in all we say and do. Paul continues to quote the promise of God for us: "'And I will be a father to you, and you shall be sons and daughters to Me,' says the Lord Almighty" (v. 18, NAS). As we learn to reverence the presence of God in our lives, He offers us the wonderful relationship of being a Father to us.

God desires to make His home in us all the time—to feel comfortable wherever we take Him. What does He do Monday through Saturday? In our business transactions? In our relationships? In our recreation? Does He feel comfortable, wanted, honored and respected? Only the Holy Spirit can create godly reverence in us that will be reflected in every aspect of our lives. The more we walk in the Spirit, the more reverent our lives will become.

⟡ RESULTS OF REVERENCE ⟡

Right relationships

The essence of worship is not an outward expression; it is a reverent relationship. As we experience this intimate relationship with God through reverential worship, our relationships with the body of Christ and with the world will come into proper balance. We will love and esteem our brothers and sisters in the church, and we will desire to see lost men and women come to know Christ. Respect for God results in respect for people. Without this attitude of reverence, we will have nothing to give to those who need to know Jesus.

Surrender

Reverence for God will also cause us to surrender our lives to Him and to live in submission to His will. We will become so aware of His presence in our lives that we will learn to truly acknowledge Him in all our ways. (See Proverbs 3:6.) The overshadowing of His personal presence is such a wonderful, satisfying experience that it will motivate us to obey God in every aspect of our lives.

As I was driving down the road one day, I thought, *Should I just waste these moments in the car, letting my mind wander as it pleases?* Just as I was determining to focus on Jesus, I heard Him say to me, "I love you." His words thundered in my spirit, creating a sense of awe. I began to cry. To think that the omnipotent God had let me hear His voice and experience His divine love for me in that moment was overwhelming. I need the love of God. I don't want to do anything that will hinder the revelation of His love to me. I believe that an increased reverence for God will bring His overshadowing presence to us in special times when we need to know His love.

Deeper worship

Cultivating reverence for God will bring us into new realms of worship. As we learn to walk in awe and godly fear, we will come to the revelation of the psalmist: "Be still, and know that I am God" (Ps. 46:10). Singing, applauding, shouting—all are biblical expressions of worship, as we will see in chapter 12. But there is a place of deep awe and reverence for the majesty of who God is where all we can do is wait in silence before Him.

In the tabernacle of Moses, when the priest entered the holy of holies once a year, he witnessed the manifest presence of God. This was not a place of dancing or sacrificing or noise. Those expressions of praise and worship were appropriate in the outer court. But in the manifest presence of God there was such awe and reverence that it evoked a deep silence. As believers, we will touch realms of worship where we wait silently in God's presence and allow Him to touch our lives in a deep and reverential way.

Victory over temptation

We will not fall into temptation when we learn to reverence God. His conscious presence in our lives will give us the strength we need to overcome every kind of temptation. As we learn to reverence the Word of God, our minds will be transformed to think holy thoughts and desire God's way above ours. Obedience to the

Word of God that gives us victory over temptation is only possible as we learn to reverence Him for who He is. As we learn to heed God's voice, we will recognize the voice of the devil and be able to overcome his temptations to sin.

Blessing

The relationship of trust that results from developing a reverence for God brings blessing, not only to our lives but also to the lives of others. When Jesus stood before the tomb of His friend Lazarus, He prayed to His Father. He asked God to raise Lazarus so that those standing around would know that God hears prayer. Jesus had such a trusting relationship with His Father that He said, "I thank thee that thou hast heard me and . . . hearest me always" (John 11:41–42). That intimate relationship of trust was not just because Jesus was the Son of God. In His reverence for the Father, the Son was completely submitted to His will and did only what He heard the Father say to do. (See John 5:30.)

Jesus walked in a consciousness of God's presence because of His reverence for His Father. When He saw the Father healing the sick and doing all manner of good, Jesus did that. He "went about doing good, and healing all that were oppressed of the devil" (Acts 10:38) because He saw the Father doing it. (See John 5:19.) What a blessing we will be to others when our lives are lived in the kind of reverence that allows us to bless the lives around us according to what we see the Father doing.

Corporate worship

Reverence in our hearts will also bring us into true corporate worship in the church. First, we need to attend the house of God to experience worship as part of the body of Christ. The Scriptures warn us not to forsake the assembling of ourselves together. (See Hebrews 10:25.) Celebrating the life, death and resurrection of our Lord in corporate worship is a divine mandate taught throughout the Scriptures.

I am concerned that there is too much of a social atmosphere in many churches when people gather in the sanctuary to worship God. Reverence and respect should characterize our corporate gatherings. The sanctuary should be hallowed as a place where the presence of God is manifest to His people. Too many people enter the sanctuary with a list of business items to discuss with members of the congregation. Others arrive and begin to visit with friends to catch up on the latest news. We need to have some convictions regarding the gathering of the congregation in the house of the Lord. We are gathering in His name to reverence Him and worship Him together as the body of Christ.

Humility

A final consideration of the evidence of reverence perhaps encompasses all the others we have discussed. True reverence clothes us with humility. The more we revere God the less self-confidence and independence we will display. We will not trust in our own abilities but will humbly depend on the Holy Spirit in all we do. A person who truly reverences God walks in a spirit of humility—waiting for Him to speak and give direction in all his ways. The prophet declared the simplicity of God's requirements for us to please God:

> He hath shewed thee, O man, what is good; and what doth the LORD require of thee, but to do justly, and to love mercy, and to walk humbly with thy God?
>
> —MICAH 6:8

Walking in humility means we have submitted our ideas and opinions to the Lord, not wanting to violate His will and desire for our lives. A study of the Scriptures reveals a powerful correlation between humility and reverence for God. Reverent hearts are humble hearts. Worship fills the hearts of the humble who know their God.

Reverent worship of God opens to us a relationship of fellowship with Him that truly satisifies the divine longing of every human heart. Understanding the nature of that fellowship will inspire us to bow in reverence before God and seek Him with our whole hearts so that we may enjoy God as He intended. Though it seems incredible that finite, sinful humans can walk in fellowship with God, the Scriptures teach plainly that God desires our fellowship.

5

Fellowship With God

A Divine Longing

IF YOU WERE TO EXPRESS TO GOD THE THING YOU WANT most in life, what would it be? For some, material things might be uppermost in their desires—a sports car, a bigger home, a Caribbean cruise, money in savings, early retirement. Others might be concerned with position more than possessions—the reward of promotion for a job well done, recognition by peers, political success, a successful career. And many would consider relationships their greatest desire—to have their ideal of family realized.

Our hearts are filled with so many desires and longings that the question "What do you want most in life?" might be difficult to answer without giving it careful thought. Whatever desire is expressed, however, even when fulfilled to its greatest potential, cannot truly satisfy the human heart. The deepest longing of the human heart is *spiritual.* Because mankind was made for fellowship with God, our soul cries out for that divine relationship, even if we are not aware of what it should be. We suffer a kind of cosmic loneliness without the attachment to God that He ordained we should enjoy.

The divine longing for relationship with God implies that the soul has a capacity for greatness. Linking the finite with the infinite—the human soul with the heart of God—opens us to true greatness through divine relationship. That relationship alone can satisfy the deepest longing of the human heart. Possessions, position, even ideal family relationships cannot bring us to the true satisfaction and greatness that we are destined for in God.

Every human spirit longs for fellowship with deity. We desire intimate knowledge of the Supreme Being— God Himself. And we feel an overwhelming need to be known by Him. Why? Because it was for that relationship that God created us. We will never find our emotional home until we learn to walk with God. We cannot expect to be truly happy until we discover the happiness of fellowship with God. Our inner cry for divine fellowship will not be satisfied until we have learned to relate to God so intimately that we have exchanged our thoughts, feelings and decisions for God's mind, emotions and will.

Although the cry for God is innate, it often remains unidentified. Many people search in various ways for meaning in life, motivated by lesser drives than the desire for God. Even in the context of the church, Christians are motivated by many of the same desires as people who do not know God. They may seek a position as a senior pastor rather than as a corporate CEO, or recognition of their ministry rather than political success. Christians' pursuits of financial goals and family relationships may even parallel those same pursuits of people who do not know God. That is not to say that these pursuits are wrong or sinful. But unless we are aware that the deepest longing of our hearts is spiritual, we may try to substitute other things for the relationship with God that will truly satisfy our hearts.

The psalmist had come to grips with this innate desire for God, as he expresses so beautifully:

> One thing I have asked from the LORD, that I shall seek: that I may dwell in the house of the LORD all the days of my life, to behold the beauty of the LORD, and to meditate in His temple.
> —PSALM 27:4, NAS

David had developed such a relationship with God that he had only one desire, one petition for God to answer, and that was to worship God and enjoy fellowship with Him all the days of his life. In Psalm 27, he goes on to tell us how he came to that conclusion. He had discovered that God would hide him in the day of trouble, give him victory over his enemies and be a father and mother to him (vv. 5–6, 10). His heart was filled with joy because of this relationship with God, and he vowed to sing his praises to the Lord (v. 6).

David gives us a secret for enjoying divine fellowship: "When Thou didst say, 'Seek My face,' my heart said to Thee, 'Thy face, O LORD, I shall seek'" (v. 8, NAS). He ends the psalm by admonishing us to "wait for the LORD; be strong, and let your heart take courage; yes, wait for the LORD" (v. 14, NAS). As we have discussed, it is the seeking heart that will enjoy fellowship with God. We have to choose whether we will focus on lesser desires or whether we will discover the deepest longing of our hearts and be motivated to its fulfillment in God.

Have you ever said, "I would give anything if I could _____"? When we make such a comment, we are usually referring to a desire we have for something we do not feel we will ever see realized. I have said, "I would give anything if I could play the piano like my friends who are concert pianists." But then I realized that was not a true statement. If I had really wanted to play the piano, I would have been willing to pay the price to study and practice until I had mastered it.

We find a way to go after what we really want. And everything we desire has a cost involved, not always in dollars, but in time, energy and sacrificing of other things to focus on that thing until we have it. A young gold medalist ice skater was asked by her interviewer what was involved in her quest to become a champion. She replied, "Six hours of practice a day every day of my life." Her entire life was focused around her desire to be a champion ice skater. She demonstrated that it was her desire by dedicating her entire life to that goal.

Do we really want to have fellowship with God? Are we pursuing the longing of our souls for relationship with Him? If so, other desires will take a lesser place, and our lifestyle will reflect that goal. To enjoy relationship with God will necessarily limit other pursuits, no matter how noble. We have to decide if we want to pursue the deepest desire of our hearts—to know God. Of course, we will still have to make a living, nurture family relationships and perhaps pursue a career. But as we pursue relationship with God, these other pursuits will not be the focus of our energies or consume all our time. We will prioritize our lives so that we can seek God with our whole hearts. As we do, we will learn to cry with David, "Teach me thy way, O LORD, and lead me in a plain path" (Ps. 27:11).

Too often Christians are double-minded in seeking God. We want Him, but we want other things, too. Other desires compete with our desire for God in such a way that they sometimes eclipse our seeking God. Wanting Him more than anything else involves our surrender of all other desires to His lordship. As we give ourselves to this lifelong process of surrender, we will be delighted with our discovery of His desires for us. Walking in the blessing of the Lord, communing with Him and knowing we are fulfilling His purpose for our lives is so satisfying that it makes all our natural desires pale by comparison.

THE SHULAMITE SEEKS HER BELOVED

The Shulamite girl described in the Song of Solomon, or Song of Songs, at one time suffered a halfhearted desire for her beloved:

> On my bed night after night I sought him whom
> my soul loves; I sought him but did not find him.
> I must arise now and go about the city; in the
> streets and in the squares I must seek him whom
> my soul loves.
> —SONG OF SOLOMON 3:1–2, NAS

She was accustomed to having her lover with her in the comfort of her surroundings. She had limited her seeking of him to a place where she had found him once—on her bed. This bed is a picture of her indolence, of her wanting her beloved on her own terms, or at least on the same comfortable terms she had once known. "Night after night" she was willing to be without his presence unless he came to her as he had done before. Finally, when he did not come, she decided she had to go and seek him where he was. When she made the effort to go out into the city, she found him again and would not let him go. (See verse 4.) She had to get out of her "comfort zone"—her own pattern, ideas and customary ways of seeking him. Finding him required effort on her part and an intensity that would not let her give up until she had accomplished her goal.

Have we experienced the presence of God in certain places or through particular devotional and worship patterns? Are we expecting to always find our Beloved there? If we are sensing a lack of His presence, it may be that He is wanting us to seek Him in new ways or with greater intensity. Our seeking Him reveals our true desire to have His presence. Perhaps He hides Himself simply so that He can take delight in our desire for Him. It is the same as in a romantic relationship. The love that motivates us to forsake other interests and pursue the affections of another—in this case, God—reveals our desire to be that other. Conversely, a lack of seeking after God reflects a lack of desire for His presence.

Many people are comfortable with religious creeds and traditions of worship, but they do not want to know God personally. They live their lives for themselves and acknowledge God only on Sunday when they repeat prayers they have learned and sing the hymns of the church. In any church tradition it is possible to learn the format of the religious services without choosing in our hearts to become deeply involved in seeking the presence of God for our lives.

ADAM HID FROM GOD

After Adam and Eve had sinned in the garden, they heard the sound of the Lord God walking in the garden in the cool of the day. The Scriptures say that "the man and his wife hid themselves from the presence of the LORD God among the trees of the garden" (Gen. 3:8, NAS). God continued to seek them out until He found them hiding there. Adam's response to God's question, "Where are you?" (v. 9, NAS), can give us some understanding of our own reluctance to be found in the presence of God. Adam replied, "'I heard the sound of Thee in the garden, and I was afraid because I was naked; so I hid myself'" (v. 10, NAS).

I heard. Sin and disobedience in our lives can make us fear the voice of God. We want to hide in our religion, our profession or our human relationships. We try to avoid the voice of God by ignoring Him or allowing our minds to be distracted by other things. In our sinful condition, we are not comfortable to come into the presence of a holy God who is omnipotent and omniscient—all-powerful and all-knowing. We pretend we do not hear Him or sense His presence.

I was afraid. Adam had walked with God before in the cool of the day. He recognized the presence of God. Yet after he had disobeyed God's command, he became afraid of Him and hid. Even Christians sometimes avoid the presence of God out of fear. When they sense the conviction of the Holy Spirit for unconfessed sin, they hide behind their excuses, intellect, opinions or tradition to justify themselves.

Perhaps there is fear of surrendering completely, or fear of what people will think if they pursue God wholeheartedly, leaving lesser pursuits behind. Some may fear they are not "good enough" for God. Others are afraid of the future or fear what they might have to give up to serve God.

I know what it is to be afraid. I have been afraid of public opinion, of the cost involved in walking with God and of giving up my religious tradition to enjoy a new dimension of the manifest presence of God. I have felt unworthy of His love and ashamed of my sin. But the Scriptures teach that God is love and that perfect love casts out fear, because fear has torment. (See 1 John 4:18.) It is through our complete surrender to the love of God that our fears, as well as other sin, can be conquered. As we open our hearts to His presence, He can change us and set us free.

I was naked. Adam and Eve lived in innocence and enjoyed the covering of the glory of God before they sinned. After their sin, they discovered their nakedness. They tried to cover themselves with fig leaves to hide their nakedness from God. Fig leaves are not a proper covering to come into the presence of God. God Himself killed an animal, shedding its blood, to clothe Adam and Eve in their sinful state.

As Christians, we must understand that it is the blood of Christ that gives us entrance to the presence of God. Human works—"fig leaves"—will never be enough to bring us into His presence. We cannot "wear" our education, our success, our religious tradition—and certainly not our sin—into the presence of God. But as we surrender to Christ, He becomes our covering of righteousness, and we need have no fear of the presence of God.

In truth, as Adam and Eve discovered, we cannot hide ourselves from God. The writer to the Hebrews understood this fact, declaring, "There is no creature hidden from His sight, but all things are open and laid bare to the eyes of Him with whom we have to do" (Heb. 4:13, NAS). The context of his statement is the wonderful benevolence of our great High Priest, who sympathizes with our weaknesses. He continues, "Let us therefore draw near with confidence to the throne of grace, that we may receive mercy and may find grace to help in time of need" (v. 16, NAS). Rather than avoid the presence of God out of fear, we can come before Him with the security of knowing He loves us and wants to redeem us from every destructive force that would keep us from relationship with Him.

✿ FELLOWSHIP IN THE CHURCH ✿

As we choose to come into the light of God's presence, forsaking our sin and other pursuits that keep us from Him, we begin to enjoy a wonderful fellowship with Him. The apostle John, the beloved apostle, reveals to us a tender intimacy that is possible to enjoy with God. In his first epistle, John uses the word *fellowship* over and over to describe our relationship with God and with God's people.

Simply defined, *fellowship* means "participation, social intercourse, communion or partnership with another." It comes from the Greek word *koinonia* and connotes true companionship and having all things in common. Having things in common means we are going to think alike, speak the same thing and do what pleases one another. We learn to have more in common with God than with the world or our own selfish desires. As we do, our fellowship increases. John declared that "our fellowship is with the Father, and with His Son Jesus Christ" (1 John 1:3, NAS). And he said he was writing about these things "so that our joy may be made complete" (v. 4, NAS). Fellowship with the Father and the Son will make our joy complete.

Communion implies a two-way dialogue of conversation and mutual affection. Whether we are referring to fellowship with God or with another person, we should not expect to do all the talking. To have true fellowship and communion, we have to learn to listen. In a friendship, if we talk all the time, we will never know our friend's heart or what he is feeling. In our relationship with God, we need to let Him talk to us, expect to hear Him and take time to listen. He may speak to us through His Word, His creation or another person. Or He may whisper a word into our hearts that, agreeing with the written Word, thrills us and gives us understanding that we needed.

The Scriptures teach that joy—fullness of joy—is the result of our fellowship with the Father and the Son. Joy does not come from attending religious services or doing good works. Joy is the result of fellowship—of walking with God and with one another. Even in the deepest, most painful trials of life, joy is an inner strength that is produced out of our relationship with God. Joy is not based on circumstances, weather or any other external condition. The Scriptures are clear that joy comes from our relationship with God.

THREE KEYS TO FELLOWSHIP

Light. John gives us three key words that will unlock fellowship to us. The first of these words is *light.* John declared plainly, "But if we walk in the light as He Himself is in the light, we have fellowship with one another, and the blood of Jesus His Son cleanses us from all sin" (1 John 1:7, NAS). God is not only *in* the light; He *is* light, according to the Scriptures. Jesus declared Himself to be the light of the world. Then He told His disciples, "You are the light of the world" (Matt. 5:14, NAS).

The psalmist declared, "Thy word is a lamp unto my feet, and a light unto my path" (Ps. 119:105). He knew that it was possible to walk in fellowship with God, allowing His Word to direct our paths. Obedience to the Word of God dispels the darkness of our souls—our minds and emotions and will—and lets us enjoy divine relationship with God. Relationship with God not only brings us into the light, causing the darkness of sin and Satan's kingdom to flee, but also causes us to be light to others walking in darkness.

Life. John declares that those who keep the commandments of God live in God, and God lives in them. Then he concludes, "And hereby we know that he abideth in us, by the Spirit which he hath given us" (1 John 3:24). Spiritual life as defined by the Scriptures involves an intimate relationship with God. Without that relationship, we do not have spiritual life. The apostle Paul declared to the Athenians, "In him we live, and move, and have our being" (Acts 17:28). It is that life of God abiding in us that makes fellowship with God possible.

Jesus declared, "I am the way, the truth, and the life: no man cometh unto the Father, but by me" (John 14:6). Life—eternal life—dwells in Christ. Only as we allow His divine life to be released in us can we hope to be free from sin and enjoy the fellowship with God that we long for.

The apostle Paul explained the mystery of this divine life:

> For the law of the Spirit of life in Christ Jesus
> hath made me free from the law of sin and
> death.... And if Christ be in you, the body is
> dead because of sin; but the Spirit is life because
> of righteousness. But if the Spirit of him that

raised up Jesus from the dead dwell in you, he
that raised up Christ from the dead shall also
quicken your mortal bodies by his Spirit that
dwelleth in you.

—ROMANS 8:2, 10–11

The Holy Spirit dwelling in us reveals to our minds
and hearts that the life of God is in us. It is His life that
sets us free from the law of sin and death. No amount
of human works could do this for us. Only the law of
the Spirit of life can defeat the law of sin and death
working in my soul. Knowledge of the Scriptures, religious traditions, good works—one of these can effect
the work of redemption in my soul that will bring me
into fellowship with God.

We must never underestimate the work of the Holy
Spirit in our lives. In my book *Presenting the Holy
Spirit,* I wrote:

As God's divine administrator of the heavenly
estates, the Holy Spirit desires to create in us the
life of Christ. In personal salvation, the life of
Christ is birthed in us. The Holy Spirit takes the
living seed of God, the Word, and impregnates
our spirits with the life of Christ. This is what
Paul declared as "Christ in you, the hope of
glory" (Col. 1:27). To experience that reality
requires personal acceptance of Christ as
the Savior who forgives sins by the power of
His shed blood on Calvary. Jesus called this
supernatural happening "being born again of the
Spirit" (John 3). We experience peace and

freedom from guilt when we are born again and begin to experience life as God intended for a child of the King to live it. To be a Christian, then, is to allow Christ to live His life through us. It is the Holy Spirit who performs this supernatural work, who makes the Word become flesh in our lives.

Then, when we are baptized into the Holy Spirit, we come into a fuller relationship with the Spirit of life. He operates in us as a dynamo of power to propel the force of His life through us. Jesus said, "But ye shall receive power, after that the Holy Ghost is come upon you" (Acts 1:8). Every aspect of the life-giving force within our inner man functions by the power of the Holy Spirit.[1]

To enjoy life in God, we must yield to the work of the Holy Spirit in our lives continually. Without life there will be no communication, no fellowship. One day as I was sitting in the beauty shop, I asked my hairdresser to do my hair when I die. She exclaimed, "Not a chance. If you want me to do your hair, you have to stay alive. I could never do it when you die because I wouldn't be able to talk to you." We both laughed, but her response illustrates the obvious: Without life there is no communication.

We need to be honest with ourselves concerning our spiritual life. If we never hear the voice of God, do not enjoy His Word, don't feel that God loves us or don't sense any communication with Him, we need to ask why. Is it possible that He is not breathing His life into us? Do we have a living relationship with God? When we are alive to God, we have fellowship with the Father and with the Son through the Holy Spirit. That communion is our source of joy.

Of course, we do not expect to have a continual running dialogue with God any more than we would with another person. We do not need to feel guilty if we are not aware of His presence every moment of the day. But as we draw near to Him in prayer and worship, seeking His face, there should be times of personal intimacy that allow us to feel His nearness and receive comfort and direction from Him. Without this communion, we can be religious, do good things, perhaps even be born again and go to heaven. But unless we cultivate a relationship with the God within who desires to commune with us, we will miss the fellowship Jesus died to give us.

Love. John declares to us that "God is love" (1 John 4:8). As we discussed earlier, love is not merely an attribute of God; love is the essence of His being, His very nature. Only as we allow the Word of God to define love for us can we learn to receive God's love and then give it to others. The world has a twisted meaning of love that is selfish at best, and no more than lustful desire at worst. To be loved and accepted is the deep longing of every human heart. Sadly, many people, including Christians, look in all the wrong places to experience love that they have defined in wrong ways. Only in fellowship with God can we experience real love as He defines it by His very character.

Keeping the commandments of God makes us friends of God. Jesus said, "Ye are my friends, if ye do whatsoever I command you" (John 15:14). Friendship with God is the highest form of fellowship we can know. Jesus defined friendship for us: "Henceforth I call you not servants; for the servant knoweth not what his lord doeth: but I have called you friends; for all things that I have heard of my Father I have made known unto you" (v. 15). The intimate communion Jesus enjoyed with the Father He shared with His disciples. They were privileged to know everything Jesus heard from God the Father.

This fellowship with divinity, sharing the secrets of God's heart, brings true fulfillment for the deepest longing of every human heart. Many people have cultivated a relationship with God that centers on themselves, their needs, their ambitions, their plans. The true friendship with God that Jesus offers involves us in the Father's interests, His plan—not only for our lives but also for the world He wants so much to reach with His love. Fellowship with God involves companionship and love that fill our hearts with joy, bringing divine fulfillment that we can find nowhere else.

Light, life and *love* are all characteristics of our relationship with God as we walk in fellowship with Him. And they become characteristics of our relationships with people also as we cultivate this fulfilling relationship with God. Our days can become a foretaste of heaven when we learn to live in harmony, first with God and then with people. This is the new commandment Jesus gave: "That ye love one another" (John 13:34). As we worship God, He brings us into fellowship with Him in light and makes possible our fellowship with others.

Learning to worship God as He has revealed for us to do in the Scriptures will help us to obey this new commandment. God has been revealing true worship to mankind since the beginning of time, as we shall see in a brief look at worship in the Old Testament.

6

Worship in the Old Testament

Progressive Revelation

THERE IS NO TRIBE OR NATION KNOWN TO MAN, HOWEVER primitive, that does not practice some form of worship. This fact reinforces the understanding that innate within every human heart is a desire—a need—to worship. We were created with the sense that there is divinity beyond our humanity. In worship we acknowledge our finiteness by bowing to divine infiniteness. Bible scholars concur that from earliest times, mankind has felt a need to worship:

> It is as natural to worship as it is to live. The feeling and expression of high adoration, reverence, trust, love, loyalty and dependence upon a

higher power, human or divine, is a necessity to man. These sentiments, toward something or somebody, and whether real or imaginary, appeal to a greater or less degree to every man. And that something determines his worship. Worship is as old as humanity. It has its root in a necessity of the human soul as native to it as the consciousness of God itself, which impels it to testify by word and act its love and gratitude to the Author of life and the Giver of all good.[1]

Idolatry, the worship of false gods, is the misguided expression of the soul of man that craves something or someone to worship. Every human heart worships at the throne of some idol—a god of human origin—until it finds the true God, who evokes true worship and gives life and satisfaction. Whether a person worships crude tribal gods made of wood or stone or sophisticated gods such as materialism, sports, intellect or marriage depends on where he is born and what his cultural values and environment teach him.

These false "gods" are almost as numerous as the people who worship them. Every person not committed to God will give allegiance and do homage to something that takes the rightful place of God. Even declared atheists worship in this sense, bowing to the finite and destructible god of self.

From the beginning of time, God has been seeking worshipers of Himself because He knows that worship expresses the right relationship of mankind to His Creator. He made us with the purpose of satisfying the longing of our hearts for Him. As we have stated, true worship is the only relationship that can completely satisfy the heart of man. Until we return to the One who made us, we will have a void inside that can only be satisfied with the presence of God. Our false gods will continue to disillusion and disappoint us, no matter how many times we exchange them for another, more promising, idol.

The Scriptures reveal a progression in the understanding of worship as men received greater revelation of who God is. Through historical events that are recorded for us, we see how men and women learned to worship the eternal God who was revealing Himself to them. Many Bible scholars divide the progress of mankind's revelation of worship into three eras, or spans, of time: *Primitive, Mosaic* and *Christian.*

Primitive era

During the primitive era of worship, we see the sons of Adam and Eve offering a portion of the product of their labor in sacrifice to God. Enos, the grandson of Adam, called upon the name of the Lord. The regular and solemn worship of God as Jehovah (that is, as the God of salvation) was celebrated in word and act— with prayer *and* sacrifice. One scholar writes, "That feeling of sonship which distinguishes man from every other creature, and not only exalts him above the brute, but completely secures him against sinking into a purely physical state of being, that original intuition of God, and that consciousness of his being dependent upon a higher power, can only be the result of a primitive revelation in the most literal sense of the word."[2] In primitive times the form of worship that Enos introduced was still maintained, for Enoch "walked with God" (Gen. 5:24). Noah was righteous before Him, expressing his gratitude by presenting burnt offerings. (See Genesis 6:9; 8:20–21.)

In a subsequent age God chose for Himself a faithful servant in the person of Abraham. He made him the depository of His revelation and the father and founder of His chosen people, who were destined to preserve the knowledge and worship of His name until the time when the Savior would come from their midst. While other nations multiplied their modes of worship according to the political constitution that they adopted and to suit the number and variety of their deities, Abraham and the posterity born to him preserved a simple form of worship, as became shepherds and in keeping with the revelation imparted to them. Wherever they pitched their tents for any length of time they built altars in order that, in compliance with ancient usage, they might call upon the name of the Lord. (See Genesis 12:7–8; 13:4, 18.) Those altars were, doubtless, simple mounds (Hebrew *bamot*) composed of earth and stone, and the animals sacrificed upon them consisted of those that were edible (that is, clean), taken from the fold.

Besides altars, memorial stones (Hebrew *massebot*) were erected by the patriarchs on spots where God had favored them with special revelations. Drink offerings were poured upon them. (See Genesis 28:18, 22; 35:14). The narrative of Jacob's vow tells of his promise that, if God would watch over him, supply his needs and bring him back in safety, he would acknowledge Jehovah as his God, consecrate the pillar he had set up, make it a house of God and render to Jehovah a tenth of all his income (Gen. 28:20–22). He excluded strange gods from his house (Gen. 35:1–4). After due preparation on the part of his household, he built an altar at Bethel.

The rite of circumcision was also added to early worship. In obedience to a divine order, and as a token of the covenant that Jehovah made with him, Abraham performed this rite upon himself and the male members of his household, commanding his posterity to carry on the tradition as an inviolable obligation (Gen. 17:1–14, 23–27).[3]

Mosaic era

When Israel became a nation with an organized civil government, in order to fulfill its divine mission it was necessary that the character and style of its worship be fixed and regulated by positive divine enactments. This did not necessitate an entirely new system of worship, since the Israelites were to serve and honor the God of their fathers. Therefore the worship introduced by Moses was improved upon and perfected only when the circumstances of the Israelites as a confederacy of tribes or a monarchy seemed to require it. It gave precise directions regarding the place of worship, including its structure and arrangements, instituting a distinct order of sacred functions, prescribing the religious ceremonies and fixing the sacred seasons and the manner in which they were to be observed. It was framed by Moses in accordance with revelation, and it recognized Jehovah as the true God.

The religion of the Old Testament is monotheism, in

contrast to the polytheism of heathen nations. Jehovah is represented not only as the only true God, as the almighty Creator, Preserver and Governor of the world and every creature, as the eternal, absolute Spirit, the good and merciful One who has destined man to enjoy the felicity of life that springs from personal fellowship with Himself, but He is also pictured as the omnipresent and near One watching over all His creatures to keep the weak and distressed. He seeks to conduct those who have wandered from Him back to the fountain of life. He selected for Himself from degenerate humanity a race to be, in a special sense, His people and to whom He, in a special sense, would be God, with the purpose of saving the world. This is accompanied with such directions for the regulations of their life that, if accepted and complied with, Israel would become to Jehovah His "own possession among all the peoples…a kingdom of priests and a holy nation" (Exod. 19:5–6, NAS).[4]

Christian era

In the New Testament, the church of Christ is not only His representative body on earth, it is also the temple of divine service continuing and perfecting the worship of the past. It embraces the principles of the Trinity and of the mediatorial work of Calvary through the Son by the Holy Spirit, and it stresses spirituality, simplicity, purity and reverent decorum. The Lord's Day and all times of holy assembly are set apart as special times of worship. The supreme means of grace are the working of the Holy Spirit through the Word of God and prayer. The celebration of sacraments such as baptism and the Lord's Supper were instituted by Jesus.[5]

WORSHIP OF A PATRIARCH

The Old Testament patriarchs learned to worship God in all situations. Their frame of reference for every event in life and in death was their worship of God. We mentioned the worshiping heart of Abraham, who willingly obeyed God when He asked him to sacrifice Isaac as an act of worship. The wonderful revelation of God as *Jehovah-Jireh,* our Provider, resulted from his explicit obedience.

The Scriptures declare of Jacob, "By faith Jacob, when he was a dying, blessed both the sons of Joseph; and worshipped, leaning upon the top of his staff" (Heb. 11:21). When Jacob knew it was time for him to die, he did not become despondent or exclaim bitterly over his plight. Death to him was no enemy. Instead, by faith, he began to bless his sons and grandsons and to prophesy the word of the Lord for their futures. Then he worshiped, leaning on his staff.

What a mantle of faith must have rested on this great patriarch Jacob when, in his dying moments, he could gather his sons together and prophesy over each one words of truth that are still being fulfilled. The Scriptures say simply, "And when Jacob had made an end of commanding his sons, he gathered up his feet into the bed, and yielded up the ghost, and was gathered unto his people" (Gen. 49:33). No fear, no struggle. He just "yielded up the ghost." May we as believers today know such victory over death and have such a mantle of prophetic anointing to the ends of our lives. Jacob understood that the passage of death is only a promotion from this troubled world to endless worship in the presence of our God.

During my years of ministry, I have had the opportunity to stand beside many people as they have been ushered into eternity. I have seen both the Christian and the unsaved person die. One of the greatest blessings a human can experience is the moment when eternity touches time and God claims him for His own. In the life of a worshiper, that moment is the most triumphant event of all. Regardless of how we enter eternity, whether through physical death or through translation after Jesus' return for the church, our greatest triumph comes when, on the wings of worship, we are ushered into the presence of the Lord Jesus Christ. There is a sacredness in death when one of God's children goes into the presence of the Lord to live eternally in an atmosphere of worship.

THE TABERNACLE OF MOSES

The tabernacle of Moses was the habitation of God when the children of Israel were wandering in the wilderness from Mount Sinai to Shiloh in the Promised Land. It was constructed of boards overlaid with various curtains and coverings and consisted of three parts: the outer court, the holy place and the most holy place. In each of these respective places, God commanded certain furnishings to be set. All had to be built according to the divine standard, the pattern the Lord gave to Moses on the mount. All were built by the enabling of the wisdom and Spirit of God.

Although I cannot give a detailed study here of this tabernacle, I want to point out the most important piece of furniture in the tabernacle: the ark of the covenant. With all its history and symbolism, the ark of the covenant was the richest of all symbols pointing to the Lord Jesus Christ. All that the ark was to Israel in the Old Testament, Jesus Christ is to His church in the New Testament. God gave instructions to Moses on Mount Sinai for the construction of the ark. It was first anointed with the holy anointing oil, and then the glory of the Lord filled the tabernacle so that no man could minister by reason of that glory.

It was here within the veil that the high priest would come and sprinkle blood upon the mercy seat once a year, on the great Day of Atonement, and make atonement for the sins of the whole nation. Christ Jesus was once and for all offered for our sins, and now we have boldness to enter into the holiest of all by His precious blood. (See Hebrews 6:18–20; 10:19–20.) The main truths represented by the ark could be summarized as follows:

- The ark represented the throne of God in the earth.
- The ark represented the presence of God among His redeemed people, Israel.
- The ark represented the glory of God revealed in divine order among His saints.
- The ark represented the fullness of the Godhead bodily revealed in the Lord Jesus Christ. (See Colossians 1:19; 2:9.)

Within the ark there were three articles: the tables of law, the golden pot of manna and the rod of Aaron that had budded. These were symbolic of the Father's law, the Son as our heavenly manna and the fruitfulness of the Holy Spirit. They also symbolize the fullness of the Godhead bodily in the Lord Jesus Christ. The ark took the central position in the march of Israel. When the cloud of glory moved, then the trumpets blew for the journeys of the camp of the Lord. Without the presence of the ark of the Lord, Israel was defeated in any battle. The church always needs the presence of the Lord in battles against the enemy if we expect to be victorious.

In order to understand the subsequent tabernacle of David, we need to realize the absolute importance of this article of furniture. Its construction and history symbolize the person and ministry of the Lord Jesus Christ Himself in the midst of His redeemed people.

To continue a chronological overview of worship in the Scriptures, we would now discuss the worship established in Israel after they became a nation and entered into the Promised Land. But because their liturgy of worship teaches us so many valuable principles, we have chosen to focus on it more closely, devoting the next chapter in its entirety to this divinely ordained liturgy. Our purpose here is to show the overwhelming centrality of the theme of worship in the Old Testament Scriptures.[6]

THE TABERNACLE OF DAVID

The central feature of the tabernacle of David was the order of worship established around the ark of the covenant, which was taken out of the tabernacle of Moses. To appreciate the new order of worship established in the tabernacle of David, we need to understand the historical events that preceded it.

God had judged the Israelites for their unfaithfulness to Him, allowing the Philistines to defeat Israel in battle and take the ark of the covenant captive. (See 1 Samuel 4.) This was a tragic day in the history of God's people. Never had enemy hands touched the ark of the covenant. The psalmist describes this historical event:

> He forsook the tabernacle of Shiloh, the tent which he placed among men; and delivered his strength into captivity, and his glory into the enemy's hand.
>
> —Psalm 78:60–61

It would be nearly one hundred years before the ark of the covenant would be restored to its central place of worship in the tabernacle of David. We are familiar with the decision King David made to bring the ark back, signifying his desire to have God take His rightful place in the center of Israel's life. At first, David did not handle the ark according to the divine pattern, however, and brought further suffering in the tragic death of Uzzah. After searching the Scriptures and discovering the divinely appointed way for bringing up the ark of God on the shoulders of the Levites, David prepared a place for the presence of God. A simple tent would house the presence of God until the building of the temple of Solomon. And all Israel gathered together in great rejoicing to bring the ark of the covenant to Mount Zion in Jerusalem.

This gathering of the people was for one purpose. The unifying factor was the bringing up of the ark of the Lord and a restoration of true worship in Israel after the sad years of decline from Samuel's time and through the reign of King Saul. The spiritual lessons are evident for the church today. If the church desires to see the restoration of the presence of the Lord through worship, then there must be unity of purpose and a true gathering together unto Him.

We must also submit to the divine order that pertains to worshiping God. The Scriptures, both Old and New Testaments, clearly reveal that God demands order in all that pertains to worship and divine service: There had to be order in the sacrifices (Lev. 1:7–8), order at the altar (2 Chron. 13:11), order at the lampstand (Exod. 39:37) and order in the priesthood (Exod. 27:21). The apostle Paul writes to the Corinthian church, "Let all things be done decently and in order" (1 Cor. 14:40). New Testament worship that includes the operation of spiritual gifts in the church must also submit to divine order.

Though we cannot go deeper into the study of David's tabernacle, one more vital truth concerning worship that it teaches us should be mentioned. Bringing back the ark of God to Israel involved making dedicatory sacrifices during the entire journey to Mount Zion. Animal sacrifices were offered in the dedication of the tabernacle of Moses (Num. 7), the tabernacle of David (1 Chron. 15:26) and Solomon's temple (1 Kings 8). Each of these dedicatory sacrifices pointed to Calvary, where the greatest dedicatory sacrifice took place. The cross was the altar to which all other altars pointed. Here Jesus Christ, the greater Son of David, offered His own body and blood as the perfect, sinless, once-and-for-all dedicatory sacrifice to God. His blood was shed for the dedication of His tabernacle—the church.

It is noteworthy that there is no account in the Old Testament that indicates animal sacrifices were ever offered again in the tabernacle of David. After the initial dedicatory sacrifices, the only sacrifices offered were sacrifices of praise and joy offered by the priests and Levites in David's tabernacle. This fact reflects the New Testament reality that after Jesus Christ was offered on Calvary, His perfect, once-and-for-all sacrifice fulfilled and abolished animal sacrifices (Heb. 9–10). The only sacrifices God accepts since the cross are "spiritual sacrifices" in His tabernacle, the church (1 Pet. 2:5).[7]

SOLOMON'S TEMPLE

The historical fulfillment of God's statutes for worship culminated in Solomon's temple. David announced to the nation that he was gathering materials to build the temple of God, but that his son Solomon would be its builder. When David made this announcement, he asked for volunteers who would consecrate their services unto the Lord (1 Chron. 29:5). He received not only volunteers but also offerings of gold, silver, brass, iron and precious stones. He told the people that he had personally given generously of his goods so that the house of the Lord could be built, and the people responded generously in kind.

This willing generosity in preparation for building the house of the Lord brought rejoicing to the people. David acknowledged that everything they had given came from the hand of God. When David finished blessing the Lord, he commanded the entire congregation to bless the Lord. "And all the congregation blessed the Lord God of their fathers, and bowed down their heads, and worshiped the Lord, and the king" (v. 20). They brought offerings and sacrifices and ate and drank in great gladness of heart. It was on that occasion that they celebrated the coronation of King Solomon, who began to reign over Israel.

The Scriptures reveal in detail the elaborate plans for the construction of the temple of the Lord. King Solomon was fulfilling the word of the Lord to David, who had wanted to build a place of worship for the Lord. When the building was complete and all Israel was gathered around, King Solomon prayed and asked God to dwell in the house they had built. The response of God to Solomon's humility was dramatic and immediate:

> Now when Solomon had made an end of praying, the fire came down from heaven, and consumed the burnt offering and the sacrifices; and the glory of the Lord filled the house.... And when all the children of Israel saw how the fire came down, and the glory of the Lord upon the house, they bowed themselves with their faces to the ground upon the pavement, and worshipped, and praised the Lord, saying, For he is good; for his mercy endureth for ever.
>
> —2 Chronicles 7:1–3

All Israel worshiped God together on that awesome day of His power when He humbled Himself and came to dwell in a temple built by man. The desire of God to be among His people and fellowship with them is so great that we see all through the Scriptures examples of His coming to them when they seek Him. Even before the coming of Christ to the earth, God was responding to the cry of His people to know Him through worship. That cry was not of human origin any more than it is in our own hearts. The desire for communion and fellowship with God is given to us by God Himself.

JEHOSHAPHAT'S WEAPON

Three armies decided to make war against God's people when Jehoshaphat was king. He sought God and called a fast among all the people of Judah. As they prayed for help against their enemies, God spoke to them through the prophet Jahaziel: "Be not afraid nor dismayed by reason of this great multitude; for the battle is not yours, but God's" (2 Chron. 20:15). While God was giving them instructions for the battle, the people fell before the Lord, worshiping Him.

Surely they had to be amazed by the instructions they received from God for winning this battle. Overwhelmingly outnumbered, they were facing certain defeat. And the Lord said to them, "Stand still! You do not need to fight in this battle!" So Jehoshaphat commanded the people to stand and praise and worship God. The Scriptures declare, "And when they began to sing and to praise, the LORD set ambushments against the children of Ammon, Moab, and mount

Seir, which were come against Judah; and they were smitten" (v. 22).

Praise and worship become weapons against enemies that are too strong for us. As we obey God's command to praise, we release God to send ambushments against our enemies and destroy them before our eyes. Then we, like the Israelites, can spend our energies picking up the spoils after the enemy is routed.

HEZEKIAH'S REVIVAL OF WORSHIP

King Hezekiah began to reign over a backslidden people after the death of his father. The first thing Hezekiah did was to cleanse the temple of God. He called on the priests and Levites to sanctify themselves to do this task, and he told them he wanted to make a covenant with God so the nation could be reconciled to Him. The house of the Lord was cleansed and put in order, and the king gathered all the people together to worship God. They brought offerings to consecrate themselves and to give thanks in the house of the Lord. (See 2 Chronicles 29:1–17; 31.)

This cleansing and repentance brought gladness and thanksgiving to the people. Right relationship with God will always be characterized by true worship of Him, individually and corporately. Today God is cleansing His church of many wrong attitudes such as prejudice, denominationalism, traditions, customs and culture. As the church submits to His cleansing process, we can expect to see a revival of worship in the days ahead.

We have not presented an exhaustive study of worship as recorded in the Scriptures. Yet the principles we explored regarding our relationship with God through worship are invaluable in helping us to cultivate that relationship. As we look now at Israel's corporate worship liturgy in the Promised Land, we can gain great insight into the heart of God regarding not only our personal relationship but the relationship of the church as well.

7

Worship in the Promised Land

A Divine Liturgy

GOD GAVE THE CHILDREN OF ISRAEL A SPECIFIC LITURGY with which to worship in the Promised Land. There were statutes and judgments to be observed when they marched triumphantly into the land of their inheritance. God promised to choose a place for His name to dwell:

> But when ye go over Jordan, and dwell in the land which the LORD your God giveth you to inherit... then there shall be a place which the LORD your God shall choose to cause his name to dwell there; thither shall ye bring all that I command you; your burnt offerings, and your sacrifices.
> —DEUTERONOMY 12:10–11

What a wonderful promise—God's presence would dwell with them in the land of their inheritance. This promise was not only regulatory for their day but prophetic for our day as well. God desires for His manifest presence to dwell in a church that worships Him in spirit and in truth. The instructions God gave Israel for worship included setting aside a day of rest, enjoying dominion over their enemies and being filled with the joy of the Lord. These injunctions should characterize our worship today.

The apostle Paul referred to the experiences of the children of Israel, declaring that they "happened unto them for ensamples: and they are written for our admonition, upon whom the ends of the world are come" (1 Cor. 10:11). This statement makes it clear that we are to learn principles of worship from the children of Israel that characterize a people living in the fullness of God's inheritance.

Change of behavior. When the children of Israel entered the Promised Land, their worship instructions required a change of behavior that would affect their lifestyle. They would live and worship under different rules than they had known in the wilderness. Moses declared to them, "Ye shall not do after all the things that we do here this day, every man whatsoever is right in his own eyes" (Deut. 12:8). The people of God were required to set aside their own personal, private judgments concerning worship in favor of a universal liturgical law. This was at once a call for obedience and for corporate unity under divine covenant. In order to bring about the rest and dominion the Lord was giving them, they had to change their lifestyle.

One change had to do with corporate worship. The inheritance and peace God gives cannot be fully realized apart from a corporate experience of worship. Individual worship, while important, must be accompanied by corporate worship in the body of Christ to fully experience the presence of God as He intended. As we obey this statute in our Christian communities, the spirit of competition will be eliminated when we realize that we need each other to enjoy the fullness of the presence of God.

During the historical period of the judges, the nation of Israel lost this corporate element of worship. The Scriptures tell us that every person did what was right in his own eyes. (See Judges 21:25.) As a result, they did not enjoy the dominion over their enemies and the rest God had promised them. The tribes evidently competed for economic and social supremacy during this time. To enjoy their inheritance they would have to become a united kingdom. Only then could they realize the worship and dominion that God had promised. They did not understand that ultimately all worship is governmental. It was not until the reign of King David, historically, that this united kingdom became a reality and worship was restored.

Destruction of idols. Along with a change in behavior, worship in the land of promise required that the children of Israel destroy all evidence of pagan worship. God commanded the children of Israel:

> Take heed to thyself, lest thou make a covenant with the inhabitants of the land whither thou goest...but ye shall destroy their altars, break

their images, and cut down their groves: for thou
shalt worship no other god: for the LORD, whose
name is Jealous, is a jealous God.

—EXODUS 34:12–14

The covenant relationship that God established with
His people provided for intimate communion with a
loving God who had subjected Himself to His own
covenant law (Num. 23:19). Any violation of this
covenant could not be tolerated by God, who would
never violate it Himself. To allow any form of idolatry—
venerating a created being or object—would bring the
wrath of God on His people. God required them to
destroy the idols they found in the Promised Land so
that they would not be influenced by them and turn
their hearts away from covenant relationship with Him.

Bible scholars trace the history of idolatry
throughout Scripture and comment on the idolatrous
bent that is common to mankind:

> There is ever in the human mind a craving for
> visible forms to express religious conceptions,
> and this tendency does not disappear with the
> acceptance, or even with the constant recogni-
> tion, of pure spiritual truths. Idolatry originally
> meant the worship of idols, or the worship of
> false gods by means of idols, but came to mean
> among the Old Testament Hebrews any worship
> of false gods, whether by images or otherwise,
> and finally the worship of Yahweh through vis-
> ible symbols. (See Hosea 8:5–6; 10:5.) And
> ultimately in the New Testament idolatry came

to mean, not only the giving to any creature or human creation the honor or devotion which belonged to God alone, but the giving to any human desire a precedence over God's will (1 Cor. 10:14; Gal. 5:20; Col. 3:5; 1 Pet. 4:3).[1]

The apostle Paul, writing by inspiration of the Holy Spirit, warned Christians against the snare of idolatry:

> When Christ, Who is our life, appears, then you also will appear with Him in [the splendor of His] glory. So kill (deaden, deprive of power) the evil desire lurking in your members [those animal impulses and all that is earthly in you that is employed in sin]: sexual vice, impurity, sensual appetites, unholy desires, and all greed and covetousness, for that is idolatry (the deifying of self and other created things instead of God). It is on account of these [very sins] that the [holy] anger of God is ever coming upon the sons of disobedience (those who are obstinately opposed to the divine will).
>
> —COLOSSIANS 3:4–6, AMP

Idolatry still separates people from relationship with a loving God. He cannot tolerate being displaced by any idol that we revere as a god in our lives. That is why worship, our true expression of covenant relationship with the living God, is as vital for believers today as it was for the children of Israel. Though the appearance or nature of our idols today has undoubtedly changed, we may be surprised to discover that people, pursuits and material things have insidiously taken the place of

God in our minds and affections. We need to allow the Holy Spirit to convict us and cleanse us, destroying our idolatrous attachments to anything that would take the place of God in our hearts.

Seeking God continually. The principle of the seeking heart is again exemplified in the worship of Israel. Life in the Promised Land was to be filled with hope— filled with expectation that God would give to the nation of Israel what He had promised. He was faithfully giving them instructions and understanding of what life would be like in the Promised Land if they obeyed His instructions. The children of Israel not only were commanded to destroy the idols of the nations living there, but also were instructed to seek the living God, who had delivered them from Egypt:

> But into the place which the LORD your God shall choose out of all your tribes to put his name there, even unto his habitation shall ye seek, and thither thou shalt come.
> —DEUTERONOMY 12:5

There is a mystery involved in this divine requirement that we seek God. Why does God ask us to seek Him? Perhaps it is as simple as the principle of human relationships: a desire to be chosen. Even between a man and a woman, the pursuit of the beloved after his lover is an integral part of a journey that culminates in a covenant love relationship. As we have seen, the heart that seeks worship brings mankind into right relationship with His Creator as well. Whether or not we can understand fully the reason for our seeking, God does require us to seek Him and gives a wonderful promise for all who do:

> But without faith it is impossible to please him: for he that cometh to God must believe that he is, and that he is a rewarder of them that diligently seek him.
>
> —HEBREWS 11:6

The antithesis of seeking God is a lack of hope or expectation of receiving anything from Him. Worshiping God is filled with promise, not only of satisfying relationship but also of receiving from Him all we need—wisdom, strength, righteousness, peace, financial provision, healing—that we cannot provide for ourselves. The Scriptures are full of promises for those who seek God with their whole hearts, learning to know Him and receiving abundantly from His hand.

Gathering. The Israelites were instructed to gather together and come to a designated place for worship. The very act of congregating is a fundamental act of worship. God had spoken to them that He would choose the place where they were to meet together to worship Him. Many Christians feel they can walk with God alone—"just me and God." While personal relationship with God does have its place, we also have to acknowledge our need of the body of Christ and seek a place of worship where the blessing of God is evident upon a congregation. As we humble ourselves to become a part of a worshiping church, we avoid the arrogance of independence that would make us do it "our way."

Bring an offering. The children of Israel were also given specific instructions concerning the sacrifices they were to make as an offering to the Lord:

> And thither ye shall bring your burnt offerings, and your sacrifices, and your tithes, and heave offerings of your hand, and your vows, and your freewill offerings, and the firstlings of your herds and of your flocks: and there ye shall eat before the LORD your God, and ye shall rejoice in all that ye put your hand unto, ye and your households, wherein the LORD thy God hath blessed thee.
> —DEUTERONOMY 12:6–7

The Word of God instructs us, as New Testament Christians, to bring offerings into the place of worship as well. Because of the perfect sacrifice of Jesus, who shed His blood on the cross, we do not have to bring bulls and goats to make an atonement for our sin. But we have not been released from the Old Testament injunction to bring our tithes—of time, talent and money—into the house of God. (See Malachi 3:10.) We are also instructed to "take with you words, and turn to the LORD" (Hos. 14:2). Thanksgiving, repentance, petition and other expressions of worship demand that we communicate with words to our God. And the New Testament instructs us to bring the fruit of our lips, a sacrifice of praise, as an acceptable offering to the Lord. (See Hebrews 13:15.)

The psalmist cried out, "So will I sing praise unto thy name for ever, that I may daily perform my vows" (Ps. 61:8). We need to bring an offering to the place of worship, our vows of consecration and service in response to the wonderful covenant of life and provision God has promised to those who worship Him. In the place of worship we affirm our relationship to God, and He does the same by allowing us to know His wonderful, life-giving presence.

Partaking of His presence. The children of Israel were commanded to eat of the meat offerings they brought into God's presence in worship:

> And there ye shall eat before the LORD your God, and ye shall rejoice in all that ye put your hand unto, ye and your households, wherein the LORD thy God hath blessed thee.
>
> —DEUTERONOMY 12:7

Rejoicing in the blessing of God is characteristic of the true worshiper. As New Testament Christians, there are several ways we can "partake" of worship. The apostle Peter admonished us, "As newborn babes, desire the sincere milk of the word, that ye may grow thereby" (1 Pet. 2:2). The written Word of God nourishes our spirits and souls, bringing rejoicing to our hearts. The prophet Jeremiah exclaimed, "Thy words were found, and I did eat them; and thy word was unto me the joy and rejoicing of mine heart: for I am called by thy name, O LORD God of hosts" (Jer. 15:16).

Receiving communion is another way that we partake of worship. Jesus gave His disciples the ordinance to celebrate communion as He partook of the Last Supper with them. He told them He would not do it again until He did it with them in His Father's kingdom. (See Matthew 26:27–29.) The apostle Paul established the celebration of the Lord's Supper for New Testament Christians, declaring, "For as often as ye eat this bread, and drink this cup, ye do show the Lord's death till he come" (1 Cor. 11:26). We experience a mystical union with Christ when we eat of His body and drink of His blood. The Scriptures warn us to examine ourselves before we partake of the communion cup so that we will not be "guilty of the body and blood of the Lord" (vv. 27–33).

The Scriptures also record the "love feasts" of the early church that brought rejoicing to their hearts: "And they, continuing daily with one accord in the temple, and breaking bread from house to house, did eat their meat with gladness and singleness of heart, praising God, and having favour with all the people" (Acts 2:46–47). Fellowship in unity with other believers in church and in our homes brings joy and rejoicing to our hearts. When we share meals together, as a church or as a group of Christian friends in our homes, we can center our conversations on the things of the Lord and reap great benefit from our fellowship together.

A lack of hunger, either for the Word of God or for communing with the saints in the Lord's Supper and in love feasts, is characteristic of a self-satisfied heart that is satisfied with something other than worshiping God. True worshipers rejoice as they "eat" the Word of God and share their lives with other believers.

Joy and rejoicing in worship. The ordinances God gave to the children of Israel for worship were given so they could experience joy and rejoicing. Though there is an aspect of our experience with God that is penitential—repenting for our sin—that place of contrition is always a preparation for experiencing the joy of worship. Repentance is not the end result of worship. If we fail to enter into rejoicing in worship, we will remain in bondage to morbid introspection that actually denies the power of God to deliver us from sin.

Joy and rejoicing are the pervading emotions of worship—the highest human expression of adoration to God. It is a result of knowing that God has defeated our enemies, who were too strong for us. After God told Jehoshaphat to "stand ye still, and see the salvation of the LORD," the people witnessed the hand of God setting ambushments and slaying the armies that had come against them (2 Chron. 20:17, 22–23). Then the people picked up the riches left by the defeated armies and "returned, every man of Judah and Jerusalem...to go again to Jerusalem with joy; for the LORD had made them to rejoice over their enemies" (v. 27). They went into the house of the Lord with musical instruments and celebrated the victory God had given them.

Worship is above all else a celebration of the risen Christ, who conquered sin and death to give us eternal life. As we apply the ordinances God has given us to live and walk in an atmosphere of worship, both individually and corporately, our hearts will be changed into His likeness, and we will enjoy God as He desires for us to do.

8

Worship in the New Testament

Glimpses Into Eternity

WHEN THE WRITERS OF THE SCRIPTURES RECEIVED glimpses into heaven, they were always met with a scene of worship. The prophet Isaiah beheld the throne of God and saw seraphim worshiping around the throne, crying, "Holy, holy, holy is the Lord of hosts: the whole earth is full of his glory" (Isa. 6:3). Worship is the atmosphere of heaven, both for the redeemed and for angels.

Although man was created a little lower than the angels, angels are still created beings who are never to be elevated above the Son of God (Ps. 8:5). Indeed, God commanded the angels to worship the Son in His incarnation: "And let all the angels of God worship him"

(Heb. 1:6). At that time the heavens were rent and the angels bowed low, pouring out their adoration upon the Lord, saying, "Glory to God in the highest, and on earth peace, good will toward men" (Luke 2:14).

WISE MEN WORSHIP

The wise men from the East who came to worship the baby Jesus remain shrouded in mystery. The Bible tells us very little about these men. Most likely they were astrologers or learned men from the Asian culture who spent their lives studying the heavens. When the star appeared, these men followed its strange movement to its resting place. We know that they were being led by the Holy Spirit. Most Bible scholars agree that Jesus must have been about two years old at the time of their visit.

These wise men must have possessed a good knowledge of the Hebrew Scriptures, for they knew they were seeking Him who was born King of the Jews (Matt. 2:2). The Scriptures reveal that it was their intention to find Him and worship Him. They carried with them gifts of gold, frankincense and myrrh, confirming their desire to worship the newborn king. They must have had supernatural revelation regarding the homage that was due this babe who was called Jesus. Surely they understood the significance of worship to have undertaken such an arduous journey to find Him and worship Him. Do our hearts burn with a desire that echoes theirs? Wise men still seek Him.

SATAN'S CHALLENGE

After Jesus was baptized in water, He was led of the

Spirit into the wilderness to be tempted of the devil. Though Satan tempted Jesus to sin in several vital areas, I believe his greatest challenge to Jesus was his demand that Jesus worship him. The devil took Jesus up onto a high mountain and showed Him all the kingdoms of this world and the glory of them. He told Jesus he would give them to Him if Jesus would only worship him.

Satan desires to receive worship that belongs to God alone. Before he fell, he was the "anointed cherub that covereth" (Ezek. 28:14). Lucifer had been the guardian of God's throne, the one responsible for the atmosphere of worship that continually surrounds the throne of God. But when rebellion was found in him, Satan declared that he would ascend and become like the most high God (Isa. 14:13–14). He is still trying to deceive men and women into worshiping him as though he were God.

Jesus' response to this temptation of the evil one was, "Thou shalt worship the Lord thy God, and him only shalt thou serve" (Matt. 4:10). He plainly declared in this statement our imperative to worship God. But His statement also makes us understand that whomever we worship, we also serve. Any idol that we allow to have a place in our lives will become our master. It is inevitable that we serve whom or what we worship. The apostle Paul confirms this fact:

> Do you not know that if you continually surrender yourselves to anyone to do his will, you are the slaves of him whom you obey, whether that be to sin, which leads to death, or to

obedience which leads to righteousness (right doing and right standing with God)?

—ROMANS 6:16, AMP

Our response to Satan's challenge of worship echoes Jesus' response: "We will worship the Lord our God and Him only shall we serve." (See Matthew 4:10.) Our service reflects our worship. True worship unto the Father will lead us to serve Him (Rom. 12:1).

NEEDY PEOPLE WORSHIP

The New Testament records that on several occasions people came to Jesus with desperate needs and worshiped Him:

> And, behold, there came a leper and worshipped him, saying, Lord, if thou wilt, thou canst make me clean. And Jesus put forth his hand, and touched him, saying, I will; be thou clean. And immediately his leprosy was cleansed.
>
> —MATTHEW 8:2–3

On another occasion "there came a certain ruler, and worshipped him, saying, My daughter is even now dead: but come and lay thy hand upon her, and she shall live" (Matt. 9:18). Jesus did what the ruler asked and raised his daughter from the dead. Once a woman of Canaan came to Him and cried unto him, saying, "Have mercy on me, O Lord, thou Son of David; my daughter is grievously vexed with a devil....Then came she and worshipped him, saying, Lord, help me" (Matt. 15:22, 25). Even though this woman was not of the house of Israel, Jesus commended her for her faith and healed her daughter.

Each of these desperate people came to Jesus, seeking His help in an attitude of humble worship. And for each one who asked for help, Jesus responded to his prayer by working a miracle and giving him the desire of his heart. Perhaps we have missed this thread of truth in our petitioning for our own personal needs. Instead of spending time begging God to hear us or trying to exercise our faith to believe an answer is coming, we need to understand that if we bow in humble worship before Him, simply expressing our need to Him, He will respond to us.

Worship is an expression of faith. Regardless of how pressing our need may be, Jesus is worthy of worship. And He responds to the petitioning of a worshiping heart. The Scriptures reveal that pouring out our love and adoration at His feet produces an atmosphere in which prayer is answered and miracles occur.

A SAMARITAN WORSHIPS

While Jesus was at Jacob's well, a Samaritan woman came to draw water. As Jesus engaged her in conversation about living water, He asked her to call her husband. When she replied that she had no husband, Jesus said, "Thou hast well said, I have no husband: for thou hast had five husbands; and he whom thou now hast is not thy husband: in that saidst thou truly" (John 4:17–18).

Jesus was not condemning this woman for being immoral. In fact, according to Jewish tradition, she could have been widowed five times and betrothed to another man. But because of Jesus' knowledge of her situation, she recognized Him as a prophet who could speak to her deepest need.

She wanted to talk to this prophet about worship: "Our fathers worshipped in this mountain; and ye say, that in Jerusalem is the place where men ought to worship" (v. 20). The response of God to her honest question shows us what to expect from Him when we come to Him in need of answers. Jesus opened her understanding about the nature of true worship and revealed Himself to her as the Messiah. She believed in Christ and spread the news to her city. Many Samaritans came to Jesus and believed in Him because of her testimony.

Jesus declared that the hour was coming when true worshipers would worship the Father "in spirit and in truth: for the Father seeketh such to worship him" (v. 23). He continued, "God is a Spirit: and they that worship him must worship him in spirit and in truth" (v. 24). True worship is sublimely spiritual—my spirit responding to the Spirit of God. Jesus' emphasis on worship in spirit and in truth teaches us that our places of worship, our liturgies and our forms and expressions of worship—all must reflect the reality of hearts worshiping God for who He is.

There is a delicate, yet secure balance between spirit and truth. If "spirit" is the anointing of God and "truth" the Word of God, we must balance between the two in order to avoid error. Some people have emphasized the moving of the Spirit of God but have neglected the truth. Others have emphasized truth without giving place to the anointing. True worshipers are those who allow the truths of God to be understood under the canopy of the anointing. They err neither by following strictly the letter that kills nor by allowing fanaticism without truth.

Our understanding of the Word of God should be continually expanding in order that every expression of our worship might flow safely within the perimeter of truth. Unfortunately, in past revivals when the Spirit of God has revealed new dimensions of truth, men have formed denominations to be the "keepers of that truth." When they camp around these facets of truth, making for themselves secure, though dogmatic, dwelling places, the balance between spirit and truth is lost. Every fresh move of the Spirit dissipates when men try to put a period after what God has done and refuse further revelation. We should ever be coming to know God in greater dimensions of truth that bring us into greater revelations of worship.

As the church receives more and more understanding of the expression of worship, we also must receive equal understanding of truth. The Father is still seeking true worshipers, those who will become vehicles of expression that satisfy His heart. As we develop our relationship of worship to the Father, our cry should be, "Father, please change me continually. I want to be a true worshiper. I want to worship You in the life of the Spirit and according to your Word."

THE SONG OF THE LAMB

The last book of the New Testament gives us a very

special glimpse into heavenly worship. Through the wonderful work of redemption, God has given all who are born again a song of worship that even the angels cannot sing. It is John the Revelator who recorded for us the powerful vision of heaven in which he experienced worship around the throne of God. As John witnessed scenes of heavenly worship, he bowed in awe.

Early in his vision, John recorded the new song sung by the twenty-four elders bowing before the throne, falling down before the Lamb and saying, "Worthy art Thou to take the book, and to break its seals; for Thou wast slain, and didst purchase for God with Thy blood men from every tribe and tongue and people and nation" (Rev. 5:9, NAS). Then he heard the voices of many angels around the throne, the living creatures, the elders and a great multitude of "thousands of thousands" saying with a loud voice, "Worthy is the Lamb that was slain to receive power and riches and wisdom and might and honor and glory and blessing" (v. 12, NAS).

This heavenly scene of worship did not end there. John then witnessed every created thing in heaven, on earth, under the earth and in the sea saying, "To Him who sits on the throne, and to the Lamb, be blessing and honor and glory and dominion forever and ever" (v. 13, NAS). And again he saw the elders fall down and worship the Lamb. When we meditate on these awesome scenes and allow the Holy Spirit to make them a reality to us, we can experience the awe of the elders bowing in the presence of the throne of God and of the precious Lamb who was slain. Our hearts should be truly humbled when we consider the cost of Calvary to bring us the gift of redemption.

After witnessing these holy scenes of worship around the throne of God, the Holy Spirit revealed to John the judgments of God that were to come upon the earth. Though there is much discussion among theologians concerning the interpretation of these judgments and the timing of them, it is clear from the Scriptures that God will judge the wickedness of mankind. A holy God cannot wink at the iniquity of those who have refused to receive the slain Lamb as their Redeemer.

Later in his heavenly vision, after the divine judgments were described, John witnessed another awesome scene of heavenly worship. In this vision, he saw a great multitude shouting with a loud voice, "Hallelujah! Salvation and glory and power belong to our God; because His judgments are true and righteous" (Rev. 19:1–2, NAS). Along with the twenty-four elders and the four living creatures who fell down and worshiped God, John heard "the voice of a great multitude and as the sound of many waters and as the sound of mighty peals of thunder, saying, 'Hallelujah! For the Lord our God, the Almighty, reigns'" (v. 6, NAS). This triumphant scene of praise and worship should inspire each of us and strengthen our faith to believe God in our present battles and trials. God wins! And we are winners with Him as we give ourselves to worship Him alone.

John records the last reference to worship in the New Testament, in which we are warned to worship God alone and not one of His angelic servants. John declared that what he heard and saw was so awesome he fell down and worshiped at the feet of the angel who showed him all these things. Then he records for us the admonition the angel gave him: "Do not do that; I am a fellow servant of yours and of your brethren the prophets and of those who heed the words of this book; worship God" (Rev. 22:9, NAS). Worship is reserved only for God, who has created all things, including the angels. As we enter into realms of worship that bring revelation of the supernatural world to us, we need to be careful not to become so awed by the wonders of this heavenly world that we forget who deserves our worship.

We will experience these scenes of worship around the throne of God one day and will praise Him for His merciful judgments along with the voice of a great multitude singing and shouting, "Let us rejoice and be glad and give the glory to Him, for the marriage of the Lamb has come and His bride has made herself ready" (Rev. 19:7, NAS). These heavenly scenes of worship recorded for us can help us in our daily walk with God to bow in awe before Him, not only for what He has done to redeem us but also for what He is going to do. Learning to praise God according to the Scriptures will give our lives a divine dynamic that will ensure our victory over sin as well as over the enemy of our souls.

9

The Dynamo of Praise

A Divine Command

WE HAVE DISCUSSED WORSHIP IN A GENERAL SENSE AS THE response of finite creatures to a holy God. It is appropriate that we, the created, should worship God, the Creator. We understand that in order to enter into the fellowship God desired with us from the beginning of time, we must become worshipers of the Lamb. There are different aspects of worship that, although they cannot be separated exclusively from one another without violating the concept of true worship, can be studied in relation to the whole to give us greater understanding of how to fulfill our destiny as worshipers.

Praise is one aspect of the worship experience for which the Scriptures give specific instructions regarding its *place, purpose* and *power* in our lives as worshipers. When we gain understanding of the importance of praising God as well as learn practical ways of praising, our worship experience will be enriched and strengthened as a whole.

The automatic response of a person when he or she is born again is to give joyous thanksgiving and praise to God. Everyone who experiences the release from the burden of sin and guilt that has tormented him all his life finds a compelling gratitude within that declares a heartfelt thank-you to God for loving him and saving his soul. This expression of praise to the living God is the beginning of a journey into praise and worship that will help us cultivate a satisfying relationship with our Creator and Savior.

PRAISE DEFINED

We have referred to praise as an aspect of the larger experience of true worship. When we look more closely at praise as defined in the Scriptures, we see a noticeable demarcation between praise and worship. Simply stated, praise and thanksgiving dwell on the things God has done, is doing and is going to do, while worship expresses our devotion to God for who He is. Praise and worship, though closely related, need to be understood separately in order to appreciate the true worship experience more fully. Praising God brings us into His presence, and worship is our heart's response to God after we are in His presence.

Marcyne Heinrichs gives us a wonderful contrast of praise to worship:

Praise enjoys God; worship esteems Him.

Praise acclaims Him; worship beholds Him.

Praise lifts; worship bows.

Praise lauds; worship loves.

Praise celebrates; worship humbly reveres.

Praise addresses God; worship waits on God.

Praise dances; worship removes shoes for holy ground.

Praise extols God for what He has done; worship extols Him for who He is.

Praise lifts us to heavenly places; worship lifts God to His rightful place—the throne.

Praise says, "Praise the Lord"; worship demonstrates that "He is Lord."

Praise is grateful for heirship to the throne; worship lays crowns at His feet.

The Hebrew language uses seven different words to refer to praise. Each has a slightly different meaning that helps us understand the precept of praise:

Towdah refers to offering a sacrifice of praise and thanksgiving, initiated by the believer, that honors God. The psalmist declared, "Enter into his gates with thanksgiving *[towdah]* and into his courts with praise: be thankful unto him, and bless his name" (Ps. 100:4).

Yadah means to praise by raising and extending the hands unashamedly unto God. "I will praise *[yadah]* thee, O LORD, with my whole heart; I will show forth all thy marvellous works" (Ps. 9:1). "Lift up your hands in the sanctuary, and bless the Lord" (Ps. 134:2).

Zamar means to touch the strings of a musical instrument. "Praise the LORD with harp: sing *[zamar]* unto him with the psaltery and an instrument of ten strings" (Ps. 33:2).

Tehillah is a word translated as song—a song of praise. "And he hath put a new song in my mouth, even praise *[tehillah]* unto our God: many shall see it, and fear, and shall trust in the LORD" (Ps. 40:3).

Halal is the primary root in Hebrew for the universal praise word, "hallelujah." It means to shine, celebrate and rejoice in the Lord with a distinct sound.

Barak refers to blessing God as an act of adoration, kneeling expectantly and quietly before Him. "My mouth shall speak the praise of the LORD: and let all flesh bless *[barak]* his holy name for ever and ever" (Ps. 145:21).

Shabach means to address in a loud tone, to shout. "Because thy lovingkindness is better than life, my lips shall praise *[shabach]* thee" (Ps. 63:3).

From these and other Scriptures we undersand that praise is vocal and physical, melodious and verbal, emotional and devotional. Praise is a release of our joy, our emotions and our souls to God. True praise is an honest response of our hearts to God. As we obey the command to praise God, we may be surprised to see the freedom it brings to our lives. Praise brings blessing, not only to God, but also to the praiser. Every aspect of praise that we see in the Scriptures can become a reality in our personal lives and in the corporate life of the praising church.

PRAISE IN CREATION

Praise can be described in the highest terms of the soul's expression:

- Praise is the poetry of worship.
- Praise is the loftiest mood of the devout soul.
- Praise is the outflow of adoring affection.
- Praise is the rhythmic language of holy joy and gratitude.
- Praise is the natural response of the soul in love with God.

The Scriptures teach that all of creation manifests the praises of God. The psalmist declared:

> Praise ye the LORD. Praise ye the LORD from the heavens: praise him in the heights. Praise ye him, all his angels: praise ye him, all his hosts. Praise ye him, sun and moon: praise him, all ye stars of light. Praise him, ye heavens of heavens, and ye waters that be above the heavens.
>
> —PSALM 148:1–4

He continues in Psalm 148 to call on the fire, hail, snow, stormy wind, mountains, trees and beasts to praise the Lord along with kings of the earth and all people—young men, maidens, old men and children. His reason? "For his name alone is excellent; his glory is above the earth and heaven" (v. 13).

The psalmists and other writers of Scripture under the inspiration of the Holy Spirit expressed exuberant songs that were no more than the cry of the seeker and the shout of the finder. They reflect a human expression of openness, forthrightness, acknowledgment of need and verbalizing of thanksgiving and gratitude to the one true God. These heartfelt responses to the God of the universe demonstrate true praise—a reverent recognition of who God is.

During Jesus' triumphal entry into Jerusalem when people waved palm branches and glorified God in fulfillment of Old Testament prophecy, the Pharisees told Jesus to rebuke His disciples. Jesus responded, "I tell you that, if these should hold their peace, the stones would immediately cry out" (Luke 19:40). Praise in the presence of God is as inevitable a response as a baby gulping its first breath to sustain life outside the womb. Being alive to God is characterized by our genuine praise of the Giver of life. As one dear old mountain grandmother of Tennessee put it, "As long as I breathe, ain't no rock gonna do my shoutin'." We were created to praise the living God.

C. S. Lewis made this profound observation regarding true praise:

> To see what the doctrine of praise really means, we must suppose ourselves to be in perfect love with God, drunk with, drowned in, dissolved by, that delight which, far from remaining pent up within ourselves, is incommunicable; hence hardly tolerable bliss flows out incessantly again in effortless and perfect expression, our joy no more separable from the praise which it liberates and utters itself than the brightness of light a mirror receives is separable from the brightness it sheds.[1]

The command to praise God is the most frequent command given in the Scriptures. The injunction to "praise the Lord" occurs over fifty times; "rejoicing in the Lord" is mentioned 288 times; and "praise" is mentioned 330 times. Far from being an option or a prerogative of ours, praise is a precept commanded by God of all who believe in Him. God does not command us to praise Him to fulfill an ego need that He has, but to satisfy the need of our hearts to be related securely and happily to our Creator, our Redeemer, our heavenly Father, our God.

It is not hard to see that praise is an integral part of our human lives. When we clap at a concert or send compliments to the chef, we are expressing a form of natural praise. Manufacturers praise their products. Parents praise their children. Fans praise their sports stars, and the government praises military heroes. C. S. Lewis comments:

> Praise almost seems to be inner health made audible...I had not noticed how the humblest, and at the same time most balanced and capacious minds praised most, while the cranks, misfits and malcontents praised least...all enjoyment spontaneously overflows into praise unless shyness or the fear of boring others is deliberately brought in to check it.[2]

Our praise and worship of God produce the "upward view" for our souls. And when we see God we are changed, as Isaiah was, in behavior, attitude and consecration. (See Isaiah 6:1–8.) Praise and worship soften our spirits, enlarge our love vocabulary and open us to the further work of the Holy Spirit in our lives. Of all the capabilities man possesses, he has none greater than the ability to praise and worship his Maker.

PERSONAL ENCOUNTER

Praise at its primary level begins with an individual sincerely communicating love and adoration to God. No matter how many people are gathered together in a corporate praise service, all encounters with God are personal. Revelation is personal. Worship is personal. Adoration is personal. Warfare is personal. These take on a dimension of power as people gather in unity and worship together, but all encounters with God essentially begin in individual hearts. Each person must enter personally into that expression of praise that the Holy Spirit is prompting. Thus, a praising church consists of individuals who praise God corporately.

The Scriptures give us beautiful examples of individuals who praised and magnified God. Mary, the mother of Jesus, after receiving a prophetic word from Elisabeth, declared:

> My soul doth magnify the Lord, and my spirit hath rejoiced in God my Saviour. For he hath regarded the low estate of his handmaiden: for, behold, from henceforth all generations shall call me blessed. For he that is mighty hath done to me great things; and holy is his name. And his mercy is on them that fear him from generation to generation. He hath shewed strength with his arm; he hath scattered the proud in the imagination of their hearts. He hath put down the

mighty from their seats, and exalted them of low degree. He hath filled the hungry with good things; and the rich he hath sent empty away. He hath holpen [helped] his servant Israel, in remembrance of his mercy; as he spake to our fathers, to Abraham, and to his seed for ever.

—LUKE 1:46–55

Mary's heart was filled with the good things God had done in the past and the good things He was doing in the present, as well as what she knew He would do in the future: "All generations shall call me blessed" (v. 48). Her prophetic song is a beautiful example of praise that results from an encounter with God Himself.

Zacharias, the father of John the Baptist, burst into prophetic praise when his son was born and he had regained his speech:

And his mouth was opened immediately, and his tongue loosed, and he spake, and praised God.... Blessed be the Lord God of Israel; for he hath visited and redeemed his people.

—LUKE 1:64, 68

The psalmist declared, "Bless the LORD, O my soul: and all that is within me, bless his holy name" (Ps. 103:1). He took personal responsibility to bless and praise the name of God. It is up to us individually to take that responsibility to express praise and thanksgiving unto God for all the good things He has done, is doing and will yet do.

CORPORATE PRAISE

As we learn to praise the Lord personally, we can enjoy the blessing and power of praising God corporately with other believers. The Scriptures testify to the great power there is in corporate praise to bring God's miraculous intervention into impossible situations. Earlier we discussed the weapon of praise that served King Jehoshaphat and the nation of Israel when they were invaded by three armies. When King Jehoshaphat sought God for help, the instructions he received from the Lord were to sing and praise the Lord and to stand still and see the salvation of the Lord.

It is important to reiterate the reality that the Scriptures directly link Israel's singing and praising with the intervention of the power of God to win the battle for them: "And when they began singing and praising, the LORD set ambushes against the sons of Ammon, Moab, and Mount Seir" (2 Chron. 20:22, NAS). These three great armies destroyed each other as God's people stood and praised God together. The people of God then spent the next three days just gathering up spoil from the slain enemies. It must have been astounding to the people when they realized the power of God that was displayed through their obedience to praise Him.

In the New Testament we see that when the early church gathered together, ministering to the Lord and fasting, the Holy Spirit spoke to them to send Barnabas and Saul for the work He had called them to do (Acts 13:1–2). In that place of corporate worship, they received direction for their lives that they so desperately needed. Our lives too can know supernatural intervention and direction as we wait before God in praise and worship.

The Scriptures declare that God inhabits the praises of His people (Ps. 22:3). We can bring the power of God into difficult situations as we praise Him. Praise releases faith in the goodness of God, the faithfulness of God and the power of God. In acknowledging His lordship over our lives and circumstances, we release Him by faith to do His redemptive work in our lives and situations. God gets glory in His church as we exalt Him corporately through our praise and allow Him to release His glory in and through us.

DIFFERENT FORMS OF PRAISE

Rejoicing praise

The psalmist declared, "Let Israel rejoice in him that made him" (Ps. 149:2). To "rejoice" means to "brighten up" (Hebrew *samach*). As we come into the presence of the Lord with rejoicing, we can expect to brighten up, to sense the light of His presence shining in our hearts. Relief from the cares of our lives will be ours as we choose to come before Him with thanksgiving and rejoicing.

Jesus instructed us, "Let your light shine before men in such a way that they may see your good works, and glorify your Father who is in heaven" (Matt. 5:16, NAS). Can the world see the light of God in our countenances as we walk among them? Our rejoicing can become a real testimony to people who walk in sadness and gloom and the darkness of sin-filled lives.

Singing praise

Singing is one of the most common expressions of praise cited in the Scriptures. Songs of praise were a spontaneous response to the goodness of God. After Barak and Deborah destroyed Jabin, king of Canaan, Deborah sang a song of rejoicing to the Lord, who had given them the victory:

> Praise ye the LORD for the avenging of Israel, when the people willingly offered themselves. Hear, O ye kings; give ear, O ye princes; I, even I, will sing unto the LORD; I will sing praise to the LORD God of Israel.
>
> —JUDGES 5:2–3

Deborah sang of the great things God had done in the past and exalted Him for the wonderful things He had just done for them. She remembered the wonderful works of God as He delivered His people from their enemies. In the midst of our spiritual battles, if we give ourselves to praise we can release our faith to believe God to conquer the enemy that is facing us by reciting the wonderful things He has done in the past. It is so important to remember the goodness of God to us and to cultivate a grateful heart of thanksgiving that we can lift to God in singing praise.

The apostle Paul instructed New Testament Christians to "be filled with the Spirit; speaking to yourselves in psalms and hymns and spiritual songs, singing and making melody in your heart to the Lord; giving thanks always for all things unto God and the Father in the name of our Lord Jesus Christ" (Eph.

5:18–20). The Holy Spirit will fill our hearts with song as we yield to Him and acknowledge His lordship in our lives. He brings the righteousness, peace and joy of the kingdom of God into our hearts (Rom. 14:17). As we allow the Holy Spirit to shed the love of God abroad in our hearts, as Paul writes about in Romans 5:5, we will find ourselves rejoicing in the goodness of God and responding to Him in thanksgiving.

Joyful praise

The psalmist David declared, "Let the children of Zion be joyful in their King" (Ps. 149:2). The Hebrew word for joyful is *giyl,* meaning "to spin around under the influence of violent emotion." It is a picture of abandon to the exuberant rejoicing we are feeling. As we truly behold our great King and learn to know Him as our mighty Deliverer and Redeemer, our souls will at times be filled with inexpressible joy and rejoicing.

The victory that only God can give us in our battles against sin, self and Satan brings wondrous, joyful praise to our hearts. We will want to respond as Miriam did when God opened the Red Sea and delivered the children of Israel from the Egyptians: "And Miriam the prophetess...took a timbrel in her hand; and all the women went out after her with timbrels and with dances. And Miriam answered them, Sing ye to the LORD, for he hath triumphed gloriously; the horse and his rider hath he thrown into the sea" (Exod. 15:20–21). Singing joyfully to the Lord is a spontaneous response of the heart that recognizes His wonderful delivering power in our lives.

Praise in the dance

"Let them praise his name in the dance" (Ps. 149:3). Though Satan has made the dance a sensual expression among the children of darkness, the dance belongs to the people of God. God is restoring the dance to His people to worship and praise Him as He has commanded us to do.

We have mentioned how David danced before the ark of the Lord with all his might when they were bringing the presence of the Lord back to Israel. To the dismay of Michal, his wife, David took off his royal robes and danced before the Lord clothed only in the linen ephod of a common man. The Scriptures clearly describe this incident of the king's abandoned praise and the reaction of Michal, along with the consequences she suffered because of her disdain:

> And David danced before the LORD with all his might; and David was girded with a linen ephod. So David and all the house of Israel brought up the ark of the LORD with shouting, and with the sound of the trumpet. And as the ark of the LORD came into the city of David, Michal Saul's daughter looked through a window, and saw king David leaping and dancing before the LORD; and she despised him in her heart.... Then David returned to bless his household. And Michal the daughter of Saul came out to meet David, and said, How glorious was the king of Israel today, who uncovered himself today in the eyes of the handmaids of his servants, as one of the vain fellows shamelessly uncovereth himself! And David

said unto Michal, It was before the LORD, which chose me before thy father, and before all his house, to appoint me ruler over the people of the LORD, over Israel: therefore will I play before the LORD. And I will yet be more vile than thus, and will be base in mine own sight: and of the maidservants which thou hast spoken of, of them shall I be had in honour. Therefore Michal the daughter of Saul had no child unto the day of her death.

—2 SAMUEL 6:14–16, 20–23

The Scriptures indicate that the reason Michal became barren, which was considered a curse in that day, was because she despised her husband as she saw him praising God with all his might before the people. Why wasn't Michal a part of the great congregation that was bringing up the ark of God to restore God's presence to Israel? Her heart seemed to be hardened to the presence of God. How careful we need to be not to allow our hearts to be hardened into a critical response to those who are worshiping God as He desires.

Praise upon instruments

"Let them sing praises unto him with the timbrel and harp" (Ps. 149:3). Playing an instrument of music as part of worship is mentioned 317 times in God's Word. By scriptural example and command we understand that musical instruments are to be used in our expressions of worship. There were many kinds of instruments mentioned in the Bible, some of which are not in existence today. The joyous sound of instruments along with praise from a worshiping heart brings honor and pleasure to God.

As we have stated, the main purpose of praise, apart from simply honoring the wonderful works of God, is to bring us into the presence of God so that we can worship Him in spirit and in truth. While entering into His gates with thanksgiving and into His courts with praise is a powerful, life-changing experience, it is only a precursor to true worship, which allows us to experience the intimacy with God that the heart of every person desires. To know God is to worship Him. And it is in worshiping Him that we learn to know Him.

10

The Value of Worship

Divine Promises Realized

As we cultivate a relationship with God through worship, we can expect to receive many promises of God that we would not otherwise receive. As in any loving relationship, there are rewards for giving, serving and even sacrificing for the beloved. Intrinsic rewards include the pleasure we experience for having pleased our loved one, the satisfaction of having served another and the joy of heart that cheerful generosity brings.

Other rewards are determined by the generosity of the loved one and the means he has to reciprocate our giving. Try to imagine the disparity between the little we can give to God and the unsearchable riches He can give to us in return. Of course, as we have seen, our motivation for worship must be our obedience to the Word of God, not a selfish desire to receive blessings for our lives. Yet the goodness of God is so great that He promises us in His Word to give blessings to those who surrender to His lordship, worshiping Him alone as God. Here are some of them:

THE MANIFEST PRESENCE OF GOD

The Scriptures reveal to us the fact of God's *omnipresence,* which means He is everywhere present, as I have previously mentioned. The Creator of the universe did not forsake His creation and leave it to chance, as some believe. He is present in every leaf and flower and is aware of every sparrow that falls to the ground. Our great God is not limited by time or space, so He constantly beholds all from His eternal perspective.

Jesus taught us concerning the *abiding* presence of God in each one who believes in Him. He taught us that just as the branch abides in the vine in order to bear fruit, we must learn to abide in Him. He is the vine, and we are the branches; without Him we can do nothing. This picture of our relationship with Christ shows us how His divine life is to flow into our lives as we learn to abide in Him. And the apostle Paul declares that we are a temple of the Holy Spirit, who dwells or abides in us. (See 1 Corinthians 3:16.) As we discussed, it is this intimacy of relationship that God has ordained for our fellowship with Him to bring us fulfillment. Andrew Murray describes this abiding presence:

Observe especially, it was not that He said, "Come to me and abide with me," but, "Abide in me." The intercourse was not only to be unbroken, but most intimate and complete. He opened His arms, to press you to His bosom; He opened His heart, to welcome you there; He opened up all His divine fullness of life and love, and offered to take you up into its fellowship, to make you wholly one with Himself."[1]

Regarding worship, the Scriptures teach us also about the *manifest* presence of God that we can experience in times of worship. I know it is unfathomable and incomprehensible to think that we finite creatures can be brought by the Spirit into the presence of the omnipotent God. But He is not only God; He is our Daddy, our heavenly Father. And there is nothing that delights His heart as much as His children pouring out their worship before His throne.

DIVINE ABILITY TO LOVE ONE ANOTHER

As we worship God, the love of God fills our hearts and gives us love for one another. This divine relationship is possible only as we walk in the light of God's Word. In the presence of God in worship, we become acutely aware of our lack of love and of any sin of bitterness or unforgiveness we are harboring against another. As we repent of our sin, the love of God is released in our hearts. The Scriptures declare, "The love of God is shed abroad in our hearts by the Holy Ghost" (Rom. 5:5).

When Jesus came with a new commandment that

we love one another, He knew that we were not capable of genuinely loving people without the love of God working in our hearts. (See John 13:34.) If we are honest, we have to admit that it is difficult to love those who do not love us in return. Even the most noble human love has a selfish element in it, a desire for reciprocity of some kind. Only the love of God is capable of sacrificing itself for another who is deemed unlovable or unloving.

We naturally love those who are loving and attentive to us and who desire to serve us. But what is our reaction to a person, even a brother or sister in Christ, who is irritating, insulting, even obnoxious? How do we respond to someone who does not agree with our opinions or honor our ideas? Are we tolerant of others' views, or do we react unlovingly when our views are challenged?

Many times we play the part of the hypocrite when we try to respond in a Christlike manner but do not have His love within that makes our response genuine. As we humble ourselves in worship, beholding the Lamb of God in all His beauty, our hearts are melted, and the shackles of prejudice, pride and other unloving attitudes are broken. In that place of worship, we can genuinely begin to "esteem other[s] better than ourselves" and find a loving tolerance for those who don't share our opinions (Phil. 2:3).

CHANGES OUR PERSPECTIVE

The prophet Habakkuk was lamenting the condition of his people, for he looked around and saw violence, law-breaking and injustice everywhere. Surveying these insurmountable problems with his natural eyes, he became discouraged. He knew he needed to hear from God, so he set himself to seek God: "I will stand on my guard post and station myself on the rampart; and I will keep watch to see what He will speak to me, and how I may reply when I am reproved" (Hab. 2:1, NAS). The guard post was the highest point on the wall surrounding the city. It was here, as Habakkuk waited, that God responded to him, giving him a vision and speaking to him personally.

God's manifest presence changed Habakkuk's perspective, and he took heart that God was going to visit His people once again. He was filled with awe as he declared, "But the LORD is in His holy temple. Let all the earth be silent before Him" (v. 20, NAS). His questions were answered, his heart encouraged and his prayer life renewed by this divine visitation. Waiting before God had brought a life-giving response to Habakkuk from God.

When God puts a desire in our hearts for something specific to happen in our lives and ministries, and then we do not see it coming to pass, we often get discouraged. And the longer we look at seemingly impossible situations and evaluate them according to our natural reasoning, the more discouraged we become. We need to do as Habbakuk did and get up to the high place alone where we can worship God.

Setting ourselves to seek God not only will change our perspective but also will bring an answer from God. He may simply speak peace to our hearts, or He may whisper a verse of Scripture into our spirits that will strengthen us and encourage our hearts. He may reassure us of the fulfillment of our desire, as He did Habakkuk: "For the vision is yet for the appointed time; it hastens toward the goal, and it will not fail. Though it tarries, wait for it; for it will certainly come, it will not delay" (Hab. 2:3). It is in the place of worship that we will find the godly perspective that will give us rest in the perplexities of life.

God's Throne in Our Midst

The psalmist instructs us to "exalt ye the LORD our God, and worship at his footstool; for he is holy" (Ps. 99:5). Worshiping God dethrones every usurper that would demand our allegiance, perpetrate unbelief in our hearts or try to thwart the purposes of God for our lives. Enthroning God in our hearts deals a death blow to our self-nature, perhaps the greatest enemy to the will of God.

I encourage you to read a psalm of exaltation every day and meditate on the wonder of who God is. It will assure you of victory over every kind of enemy that wants to dethrone the King of kings in your life. God's presence will be made known in our worship, individually and corporately. And where He is, there is life—eternal life, abundant life—and victory over every kind of "death."

Unity in the Body of Christ

True unity in the body of Christ will come only through worship. As we worship God together, our eyes are lifted above our human pettiness, prejudice and differences of every kind. We cannot see the barriers that separate us when we are beholding His face together. In the miracle of corporate worship, every person can grow together as wheat in a field and thrive in the life-giving atmosphere worship creates.

The prophets described the wonderful unity the body of Christ would one day enjoy. In his prophetic vision of the army of the Lord Joel declared:

> Blow ye the trumpet in Zion, and sound an alarm in my holy mountain: let all the inhabitants of the land tremble: for the day of the LORD cometh, for it is nigh at hand.... They shall run like mighty men;... they shall march every one on his ways, and they shall not break their ranks: neither shall one thrust another; they shall walk every one in his path.
>
> —JOEL 2:1, 7–8

Joel was comparing the church to a military host marching in complete harmony. In an army, the life of the whole depends on each individual's doing his duty. Daily discipline and precise training, individually and corporately, is required for the objective of victory to be realized. We cannot allow jealousy, envy, bitterness, competition, strife, unforgiveness or other sins to separate us. This is akin to thrusting each other through with unkind words, attitudes and actions.

The love of God that is manifest as we worship together will replace the hatred that brings division and fosters a sectarian spirit, even between denominations. The apostle Paul used the analogy of the body to describe the unity the church must have to be victorious. The goal is that, "speaking the truth in love, [we all] may grow up into him in all things, which is the head, even Christ: From whom the whole body fitly joined together and compacted by that which every joint supplieth, according to the effectual working in the measure of every part, maketh increase of the body unto the edifying of itself in love" (Eph. 4:15–16).

Of course, unity is a supernatural work of the Holy Spirit. It is impossible for men to create unity without the love of God being shed abroad in our hearts by the Holy Ghost. (See Romans 5:5.) The prophet Isaiah saw an interesting picture of the unity God would create:

> I will open rivers in high places, and fountains in the midst of the valleys: I will make the wilderness a pool of water, and the dry land springs of water. I will plant in the wilderness the cedar, the shittah tree, and the myrtle, and the oil tree; I will set in the desert the fir tree, and the pine, and the box tree together: that they may see, and know, and consider, and understand together, that the hand of the LORD hath done this, and the Holy One of Israel hath created it.
>
> —ISAIAH 41:18–20

Every nurseryman understands the impossibility of planting trees together that require different climatic conditions to thrive. Every kind of tree needs different types of soil, levels of moisture and ranges of temperatures in which to grow. Yet God proclaimed that He was going to bring the waters of life to the wilderness and the desert and plant every kind of tree there together. And He declared that people would then understand that the Lord Himself had created it.

That same supernatural power of God will be necessary to create unity in the body of Christ. As we allow the waters of the Spirit to flow out of us in worship, we will begin to see greater unity in the body of Christ. In the Scriptures we are referred to as trees of righteousness, the planting of the Lord. (See Isaiah 61:3.) When He plants us, we will thrive and grow no matter who is "planted" next to us.

Paul declared, "But now hath God set the members every one of them in the body, as it hath pleased him" (1 Cor. 12:18). When we humble ourselves in worship, we will learn to esteem others better than ourselves and preserve the unity of the body of Christ (Phil. 2:3). Our opinions, prejudices—even our theology—will not be able to break the unity that God works in our hearts as we worship before His throne in deep humility.

A WEAPON IN SPIRITUAL WARFARE

The psalmist praised and blessed the Lord for giving him power over his enemies: "Blessed be the LORD my strength, which teacheth my hands to war, and my fingers to fight" (Ps. 144:1). David was involved in fighting armies that wanted to destroy the nation of Israel. As Christians, we understand that we are in spiritual warfare against principalities and powers that want to destroy the body of Christ:

> For we wrestle not against flesh and blood, but
> against principalities, against powers, against the
> rulers of the darkness of this world, against spir-
> itual wickedness in high places.
>
> —EPHESIANS 6:12

The place of worship equips us as warriors against the attacks of the evil one, who wants to destroy the lives of believers as well as those who do not know Christ. Satan hates our worship because he knows the power of it to put him to flight. Praise and worship become a fortress for us against the enemy. Isaiah declared, "Thou shalt call thy walls Salvation, and thy gates Praise" (Isa. 60:18). We can assume a victorious position through worship, making war in high places.

As we lift our hands in praise and surrender to God, acknowledging His lordship over our lives, we acknowledge the defeat of Satan as well. While we cannot hope to gain victory over an unseen spiritual enemy in our own strength, we can indeed be victorious as we learn to use the spiritual weapons of prayer and praise.

One of Satan's most effective devices is to attack our thoughts, causing us to imagine all kinds of ungodly ideas. How often have you been tormented by feelings of unworthiness, guilt or just vague uneasiness concerning your relationship with God? Worship becomes a spiritual weapon that pulls down the enemy's strongholds in our imagination, bringing our thoughts into line with the Word of God. The apostle Paul described this warfare:

> For the weapons of our warfare are not carnal,
> but mighty through God to the pulling down of
> strong holds; casting down imaginations, and
> every high thing that exalteth itself against the
> knowledge of God, and bringing into captivity
> every thought to the obedience of Christ.
>
> —2 CORINTHIANS 10:4–5

Worship is a mighty weapon in our arsenal that releases the power of God to deliver us from our enemies and fill our thoughts with the goodness of our God. Our whole lives revolve around the centrality of worship that brings us continually into right relationship with God.

We could not possibly articulate all the profitable values of worship as they are revealed in the Word of God. But we can conclude that worship is central to our learning to enjoy the abundant life that Jesus came to give us. For all eternity, we will be coming to know the Lord, and our worship will be deepening with each new revelation of God. We can deepen our worship experience here on earth as we learn to understand the things that can hinder it.

11

Hindrances to Worship

Breaking the Barriers

PART OF THE PROCESS OF GROWING INTO A MATURE relationship with God through worship involves understanding hindrances to that relationship. As we become aware of the things that hinder our worship, we will learn to break the barriers they create that keep us from enjoying relationship with God. Let's look at several of them.

SIN

The presence of sin in our lives can hinder our worship. The psalmist cried, "If I regard iniquity in my heart, the Lord will not hear me" (Ps. 66:18). And the prophet Isaiah declared, "Your iniquities have separated between you and your God, and your sins have hid his face from you, that he will not hear" (Isa. 59:2). Regarding iniquity does not mean just discovering it; the term implies that we persist in living with it though we know it is there.

While the Scriptures do not teach that we must be sinless to enter into worship, they are clear that we must be willing to repent of known sin in order to walk in fellowship with God. Repentance must become a lifestyle for the believer so that we can be continually cleansed from sin as we are convicted by the Holy Spirit. We learn to live in dependence on the wonderful blood of Jesus, as Peter admonishes us: "Forasmuch as ye know that ye were not redeemed with corruptible things, as silver and gold, ... but with the precious blood of Christ, as of a lamb without blemish and without spot" (1 Pet. 1:18–19).

The Word of God is clear that we are set free from the guilt of sin, the power of sin and the penalty of sin through the precious blood of Christ:

- *The guilt:* "There is therefore now no condemnation to them which are in Christ Jesus, who walk not after the flesh, but after the Spirit" (Rom. 8:1).
- *The power:* "For sin shall not have dominion over you" (Rom. 6:14).
- *The penalty:* "Being now justified by his blood, we shall be saved from wrath through him" (Rom. 5:9).

Jesus effectively dealt with sin in all its aspects on

Calvary. We are free to choose to enjoy freedom from sin and enter into a wonderful life of fellowship with God through worship. Repenting quickly for any sin that the Holy Spirit shows us will ensure our liberty in worship.

FEAR

Earlier I pointed out Adam's fear of the presence of God after Adam had disobeyed the command of God. I suggested various causes of fear, but my list could be added to indefinitely. There are almost as many kinds of fear as there are people who suffer from them. Few emotions immobilize and so greatly incapacitate a person as fear. Fear arrests sound reasoning, anesthetizes the senses and exercises censorship over our wills.

The Word of God teaches us how to overcome fear: "There is no fear in love; but perfect love casteth out fear: because fear hath torment. He that feareth is not made perfect in love" (1 John 4:18). Learning to abide in the love of Christ through our worship of Him displaces the torment of fear. As a trusting relationship with God deepens, we will discover that the fear that once governed us has no power over us anymore. How many times Jesus declared "Fear not" to His disciples and others while He walked on the earth. His loving command is the same to us today.

SELF-EGO

A self-centered person does not seek to worship; such a person expects to be revered himself. The self-abasing person has equal difficulty, for whether our attitude is "I am great" or "I am worthless," the fundamental message is still "I am." Such egocentricity precludes the humble attitude that desires to worship the great I AM.

The apostle Paul admonished us, "For I say . . . to every man that is among you, not to think of himself more highly than he ought to think; but to think soberly, according as God hath dealt to every man the measure of faith" (Rom. 12:3). In Christ, we neither exalt nor abase ourselves. We think of ourselves, rather, according to what God has done for, in and through us. Worship does not correspond to us; it corresponds exclusively to God.

THE PHARISAICAL SPIRIT

Jesus was invited to dine as a guest in the house of a Pharisee. During dinner, Mary, who was undoubtedly not invited, entered the house to anoint Jesus with a costly ointment and to worship Him. The Pharisee condemned Mary as a sinner. Filled with his own ideas of what was right and wrong, he condemned Jesus also, because He had allowed this sinful woman to touch Him. The Scriptures say that the Pharisee "spake within himself" (Luke 7:39). Not daring to express aloud his negative reaction to the situation, he nevertheless reasoned according to his legalistic mind and accused the Master and the woman who worshiped Him.

How often does the "Pharisee" spirit express itself in our hearts? That condemning spirit is one of the major hindrances to our own worship and often tempts us to despise the reality of worship. We need to recognize the source of this diabolical attitude and learn how to be delivered from it so that we can become true worshipers.

Worship was the central issue in the biblical account of the first occasion in which this pharisaical spirit was manifested. Adam's son Cain, the first murderer in the world, manifested this spirit toward his brother Abel. Cain became angry with Abel when God accepted Abel's offering of worship but did not accept his own. The New Testament tells us, "By faith Abel offered unto God a more excellent sacrifice than Cain, by which he obtained witness that he was righteous" (Heb. 11:4). Cain hated Abel because his righteousness was accepted by God.

God spoke to Cain, asking him why he was angry and assuring him that if he did well, he would be accepted. He told him also that if he did not do well, sin was lying at the door. (See Genesis 4:3–7.) God gave Cain an opportunity to repent, but Cain persisted in his own way and hated his brother, who had pleased God with his worship.

That first murder was typical of the Pharisees' desire to kill Jesus, the Righteous One. The Pharisees hated Jesus because they had made an idol of religion and had rejected the true righteousness of the Scriptures. Jesus said to them, "You search the Scriptures, because you think that in them you have eternal life; and it is these that bear witness of Me; and you are unwilling to come to Me, that you may have life" (John 5:39–40, NAS). They preferred to receive honor from one another and to rule over others by their traditions rather than to receive the life that Jesus offered them.

Jesus attributed their unbelief to their desire to receive honor from men: "How can ye believe, which receive honour one of another, and seek not the honour that cometh from God only?" (John 5:44).

Jesus was tolerant of sinners who came to Him, but He had no tolerance for the Pharisees. The Pharisees and doctors of the law were the only ones for whom He did not have one kind word. He didn't bless them; He pronounced woe upon them, calling them whited sepulchres and murderers like their father, the devil. (See Matthew 23:27; John 8:44.) His evaluation proved to be correct, for they were the ones who later crucified Him. Pilate, a pagan ruler, observed that "for envy" they had condemned Jesus to death (Matt. 27:17–18).

The pharisaical spirit militates against true worship and relationship with God. But Jesus warned the Pharisees: "Woe unto you…Pharisees, hypocrites! for ye shut up the kingdom of heaven against men: for ye neither go in yourselves, neither suffer ye them that are entering to go in" (Matt. 23:13). People who are ruled by a pharisaical spirit today love the praises of men. They are very concerned about position and honor. They insist on ruling over people with their church traditions and laws. They are not impressed with the humble way that Jesus came, healing the sick and feeding the multitudes. They are content to receive glory themselves for their feigned righteousness.

The pharisaical spirit is one of the greatest abominations that has ever invaded the church. People who are ruled by this attitude masquerade as being "superspiritual." There is no such thing as superspiritual—for no one can have too much of God. But there are many people who have too much of religion. To be "super-religious" is not the same as being truly spiritual. A spiritual person is characterized by the humility of a worshiping heart. Only those who allow the nature of Christ to be seen in their attitudes, words and conduct are truly spiritual.

The intent of the pharisaical spirit is to kill the Christ-life in each one of us. The first place to look for this spirit is within our own self-life. We resist the idea that our flesh is religious. But unless we yield to the Christ-life within us, it is simply human nature to be religious. When we humble ourselves to receive the Word of God joyfully, we will learn to guard against the characteristics of the pharisaical spirit I am describing.

The pharisaical spirit wrongly esteems the written Word above the living Word. It worships the Book of the Lord instead of bowing to the Lord of the Book. The Pharisees were given primary responsibility for maintaining the integrity of the written Word through centuries of copying and recopying. We owe them much for their diligence. But in their zeal to protect the Scriptures from abuse, the Pharisees implemented a system of interpretation based more on their own traditions than on the actual text.

The modern counterparts of the Pharisees of Jesus' day still try to protect the Scriptures from doctrinal abuse. They have created an intricate system of interpretation to try to protect the integrity of their doctrine. Their rigidity, however, will radically limit any further revelation they might otherwise receive. They fight for the truth, yet miss the fresh visitation of the Holy Spirit during revival because His progressive revelation transcends their doctrinal understanding.

Everyone who loves the truth desires sound doctrine also. But sound doctrine, though important, is not meant to be an end in itself. Adopting such a position results in arguments among brethren and divisions in the body of Christ. Sound doctrine is meant to teach us how to be conformed to the image of Christ. It enables us to determine the will of God so that we can obey Him. Doctrine must remain an instrument in the hands of the Holy Spirit, or it becomes a weapon for use by the carnal mind.

It is possible to memorize the entire Bible and still not know the Truth. Truth is a Person. While it is true that we cannot love God without loving His Word, it is also true that to elevate the written Word above God Himself makes an idol out of the Scriptures. If that happens, we allow the Scriptures to supplant our relationship with God.

Developing a personal relationship with God the Father, God the Son and God the Holy Spirit—this priceless gift of the Lord to His people—is the truth that will set us free from the bondage of legalism. Christians should search the Scriptures to find the God of the Scriptures and not miss His visitation as the Pharisees did. Jesus Himself declared the end of the Pharisees in the great Magna Carta of the gospel, the Beatitudes. He warned, "For I say unto you, That except your righteousness shall exceed the righteousness of the scribes and Pharisees, ye shall in no case enter into the kingdom of heaven" (Matt. 5:20).

The pharisaical spirit will never enter the kingdom

of heaven. It is high-minded and proud. We must guard our hearts against this wicked spirit or lose the kingdom of God. It was the pharisaical spirit that killed Jesus. That same spirit is determined to destroy the Christ that lives in you. As a Spirit-filled believer, stand and declare boldly, "His house will be a house of prayer, purity, power and holiness!" We must become worshipers and rebuke the host Pharisee that condemns worship. Pure spiritual worship is not only a place of fulfillment of our divine destiny, it is also a place of safety from the proud pharisaical spirit and all other forms of deception. Becoming a true worshiper is not an option; it is a mandate for every believer.

THE "BUSY" SYNDROME

One of the greatest hindrances to becoming a worshiper is lifestyle. As born-again Christians, how can we justify a lifestyle that is so filled with activities that we have no time to wait before God in worship? The sad confession of many ministers and church staff is that they are so busy with programs and worthwhile projects that they have no time for personal devotional prayer and reading the Word. We cannot cultivate relationships on the human level without giving them proper time and attention. How much less can we cultivate our relationship with God without dedicating time daily to fellowship with Him.

We are familiar with the biblical account of Jesus going to visit His friends in Bethany. Martha was busy working while Mary sat at the feet of Jesus. The Scriptures say that Martha was distracted by all the preparations that had to be made. She asked Jesus, "Lord, don't you care that my sister has left me to do the work by myself? Tell her to help me!" (Luke 10:40, NIV).

Jesus' response reveals once again God's priority of relationship over work: "'Martha, Martha,' the Lord answered, 'you are worried and upset about many things, but only one thing is needed. Mary has chosen what is better, and it will not be taken away from her'" (vv. 41–42, NIV). Jesus regards our *communion with Him* as much more important—the one thing that is needful—than our *work for Him.* If our work distracts us from Him we can expect to receive the same rebuke Martha did.

In each one of us dwell a Mary and a Martha. As our Christian life progresses, one or the other will take pre-eminence as a result of our values and perspective of "success." In our culture, with our religious heritage, it is usually Martha who prevails. How easy it is for those in Christian service to gradually, almost imperceptibly, allow their work to crowd out their relationship with the Lord.

The apostle Paul warns us that as soldiers of Christ Jesus we should not allow ourselves to be caught up and distracted by "civilian" (worldly) affairs. (See 2 Timothy 2:4, NIV.) The good things are those that most often distract us. Doing the work of the Lord many times displaces the Christian leader's personal prayer relationship with Jesus. Making a good living for the family means working long hours and leaving no time or energy to spend with God.

We may secretly sympathize with Martha in her desire to make sure that her house looked nice and that a tasty meal was made ready for Jesus. His response to Martha's pursuits, however, was to declare that they were distractions from her first goal, that of relationship with Him. Nothing is important enough to take priority over our relationship with Him. God values our fellowship with Him more than anything we can or will ever do for Him.

Of course, either-or people would gladly hear the message that we are not to work for the Lord at all but to give ourselves entirely to worship Him and fellowship with Him. Jesus was not disclaiming work when He rebuked Martha; He was simply saying that work had become a worrisome distraction to her. To be distracted means to be drawn away or diverted from one's primary goal. Work had taken the wrong priority in Martha's life, causing her to miss the relationship with Jesus that Mary was enjoying with Him. As we pursue relationship with God, He has promised to show us how to live: "In all thy ways acknowledge him, and he shall direct thy paths" (Prov. 3:6).

THE DECEITFULNESS OF RICHES

In the parable of the sower who sowed the seed of the Word of God, Jesus taught us about another hindrance to relationship with God. In the parable, some of the seeds sown fell among thorns. The thorns represent the worries of this life and the deceitfulness of wealth. They spring up and choke the Word of God so that it has no effect in the life of the one who is consumed with them. (See Matthew 13:22.) Jesus had more to say about money than almost any other subject. He knew the power that money and the love of money wield over people. On one occasion Jesus declared that no man could serve two masters, God and mammon (riches). He clearly taught that money would vie for lordship over our lives with the one true Lord, Jesus Christ.

Money is one of the greatest idols to which man has bowed and has given his life to serve. It offers power, comfort and fulfillment of men's desires for pleasure. It seems to bring with it honor and respect as well. But the Bible refers to the deceitfulness of riches. There is a lie in material wealth that convinces people they are better than those who do not have it. Wealth also promises satisfaction that it cannot give, for the human heart will never be satisfied with anything money can buy.

The Scriptures declare, "For the love of money is the root of all evil: which while some coveted after, they have erred from the faith, and pierced themselves through with many sorrows" (1 Tim. 6:10). The root of all evil lies not in money itself but in the covetous heart that sets its affections on it. Money cannot buy anything that is eternal. And only that which is eternal will truly satisfy our hearts. We were made for relationship, fellowship and communion with God, who alone must be worshiped.

SATANIC INTERFERENCE

Satan knows that our "high praises" and worship can defeat his destructive purposes to frustrate the Word of God (Ps. 149:6). As believers, we do not need to be subject to Satan's devices. The Scriptures instruct us to submit ourselves to God and resist the devil, promising that if we do this, he will flee from us (James 4:7). The fact that we are instructed to resist him confirms that he will try to resist us in our efforts to worship God.

It is our submission to God, first of all, that keeps us safe from the "wiles of the devil" (Eph. 6:11). If we live in surrendered worship of God, we will have the power to resist the enemy in our lives and know that he is defeated. When we lift the name of Jesus over our situations, we will experience the victory He promised: "That through death he might destroy him that had the power of death, that is, the devil" (Heb. 2:14).

As we cultivate pure spiritual worship, sin and the Pharisee—as well as the workaholic, the lover of money and any other idolatrous thing in us—will be exposed. In the place of worship we can be delivered from all barriers to a satisfying relationship with God and a discovery of our personal destiny in Him. We can join with the community of believers to experience corporate worship that not only gives satisfaction in expression of worship but also helps to frustrate the working of the enemy in the earth.

12

Corporate Worship

Biblical Expressions in Worship

THE CHURCH—DESCRIBED IN SCRIPTURE AS THE BODY OF Christ—has been given the awesome privilege and responsibility of expressing true worship of our infinite God in the earth. As diverse as the body of Christ is, represented by many church traditions of true believers, so diverse are the expressions of worship. Yet wherever sincere hearts are bowing before God in worship, the Lord Himself has promised to be there. Where the Spirit of the Lord breathes His life into liturgy, sacraments, the Word, prayer and musical expressions, faithful hearts lift praise and worship corporately unto God.

We have discussed the central themes of worship,

defining it comprehensively as a life that is surrendered to the lordship of Christ and exploring many aspects of worship as revealed in the Scriptures. No study of true worship would be complete, however, without considering the practical expressions of corporate worship, especially as set forth in God's Word. While it is the heart of the individual believer that must respond to God in worship, it is the church corporately that represents the revelation of Christ most fully in the earth. There is a supernatural dynamic of corporate worship taught in the Scriptures that fulfills the purposes of God in the earth in a way that would not otherwise be realized.

Although I cannot present an in-depth study of the New Testament teaching concerning the church, I must begin with the assumption that the work of the Holy Spirit focuses on preparing the people of God to be a holy bride for the Son of God. Some have described the church as the crown jewel of the work of Calvary—the precious divine treasure that God is forming that will dwell with Him. The apostle Peter declared to the church, "But ye are a chosen generation, a royal priesthood, an holy nation, a peculiar people; that ye should shew forth the praises of him who hath called you out of darkness into his marvellous light" (1 Pet. 2:9).

The light of God will shine through His people as we demonstrate the praises of God in the earth. This is a corporate responsibility of a people "which in time past were not a people, but are now the people of God" (v. 10). While the Scriptures teach that it is our very lives that are to show forth God's praise in the earth, they also give instruction for the corporate expression of praise as we worship God together.

We have defined worship in spirit and in truth simply as the expression of a heart yielded to the Holy Spirit and worshiping according to the truth of the Word. It involves believers honoring and adoring God as the Holy Spirit inspires them according to the pattern He has revealed to us in the Scriptures. Without yielding to the quickening of the Holy Spirit, worship is a lifeless form, for "the letter killeth" (2 Cor. 3:6). But without submitting to the truth of the Word, we are in danger of becoming involved in sentimentalism, emotionalism and even fanaticism. For that reason it is vital that we create a balance in worship that the Scriptures define as worship in spirit and in truth.

Just as in the beginning of time, when the Spirit and the Word brought order out of chaos, both the Spirit and the Word must be present in our worship expressions for divine order to be estblished. The Spirit brooded over the face of the earth, and the Word spoke order into creation. (See Genesis 1:1–5.) So divine worship is dependent upon the Spirit and the Word operating in the midst of the worshiping congregation.

When we studied the nation of Israel and the liturgy God gave them for worship in the Promised Land, we outlined principles of corporate worship that are valid for us today. There are some who believe that corporate worship in general, and the musical expression of worship specifically, were only for Old Testament times. They do not see specific instruction in the New Testament for the jubilant celebrations of singing, dancing and playing of instruments that the Old Testament records.

We need to understand that the references in the New

Testament regarding worship expressions assume the knowledge and acceptance of Old Testament practices, since these were the Scriptures early Christians had to follow. It would be too great an assumption to consider that all the Old Testament worship forms were somehow abolished for New Testament Christians, even though there were no explicit instructions for them to be eliminated. As we look more closely at worship in the early church, we will see that many corporate expressions of worship were taught and practiced.

SINGING

One of the most poignant occasions for worshiping in song occurred at the Last Supper. Matthew and Mark record that Jesus and the disciples sang a hymn after Jesus had instituted the sacrament we call communion, breaking the bread and drinking the cup that represented His body and blood. Have you ever wondered what they sang? On this momentous occasion, filled with a dreaded anticipation of what was about to happen to their Lord, the disciples followed Jesus as He directed them to sing a hymn.

The Greek word translated "hymn" *(humneo)* means "to sing a religious ode," which, by implication, meant "to celebrate God in song," perhaps by singing one of the psalms set to music. Some scholars reason that they must have sung the "Great Hallel," or "Paschal Hymn," which was usually sung after Passover by the Jews (Ps. 113–118). Whatever the content, Jesus was surely teaching by example the way we should celebrate His death, as the apostles taught later in the Scriptures.

Corporate Worship

Even in times of great trial it is appropriate to celebrate God, worshiping Him corporately in song.

The apostle Paul, writing specifically concerning the proper order of worship for the Corinthian church, encouraged the people to sing psalms along with other public forms of edification. (See 1 Corinthians 14:26.) The word translated psalm *(psalmos)* from the Greek means a set piece of music accompanied by the voice, harp or other instrument.

Again, Paul instructs the church at Ephesus to sing psalms, hymns and spiritual songs and to make melody in their hearts unto the Lord (Eph. 5:18–19). He declares that it is a natural part of living the Spirit-filled life to worship God in song. Inherent in the Greek meaning of the word *psalm (psallo)* is the understanding of twitching or twanging, playing on a stringed instrument.

We can assume that they sang their praises corporately, accompanied by a kind of stringed instrument that has been lost in antiquity.

When Paul and Silas were severely beaten and thrown into the innermost dungeon, their hands and feet in stocks, their backs bleeding, they began to sing praises to God at midnight. If this qualifies as a corporate worship service, with only two voices raised to God, it is perhaps the smallest one recorded. But the miraculous intervention of God into their desperate situation is worthy of mention. It seems that He responded immediately and powerfully to their songs of praise, which were offered sacrificially in spite of their pain and dreadful circumstances. Not only did they receive personal deliverance as a result of their worship, they brought the message of salvation to the entire household of the jailer as well.

Paul and Silas praised God in the midst of their trial, and God honored them by acting supernaturally to deliver them. Jesus promised that where two or three are gathered together in His name, He will be there with them. (See Matthew 18:20.) As Paul and Silas experienced the powerful presence of Christ with them in that terrible place, so we can expect to know the delivering presence of God as we dare to sing praises to Him in our darkest hour.

There is an interesting reference in the Book of Hebrews to a messianic prophecy from Psalm 22:22: "I will declare thy name unto my brethren, in the midst of the church will I sing praise unto thee" (Heb. 2:12). Jesus Himself, who "is not ashamed to call [us] brethren" (v. 11), declared that He would sing praise to the Father in the midst of His worshiping people. Have we understood the spiritual impact of singing praise to God that allows the Son of God to join with us as we worship the Father? It is this communion of divine fellowship that God desires for His people.

Other New Testament references to worship in song include the apostle Paul's declaration that he would sing with the spirit and also with the understanding (1 Cor. 14:15). In context, he seems to be referring to singing in tongues by the inspiration of the Spirit, as well as singing in a language he understood. And we have discussed John's vision of worship around the throne, in which the four beasts and the elders sang a new song accompanied by harps (Rev. 5:8–9) and "them that had gotten the victory over the beast" sang the song of Moses and of the Lamb (Rev. 15:2–3). For those of us who especially love the sound of choral music, we can only imagine the sound of thousands of voices singing their adoration in the presence of God Himself. Surely we can enter into new realms of corporate worship in song in the church as we allow our faith to be released through songs of praise.

When we follow the instructions of Paul to "let the word of Christ dwell in [us] richly in all wisdom; teaching and admonishing one another in psalms and hymns and spiritual songs, singing with grace in [our] hearts to the Lord" (Col. 3:16), we can expect our corporate worship services to be elevated to a prophetic anointing. The Word of God, expressed in song, will bring life—the quality of eternal life—into our churches. Today, many songs are being written using only Scriptures as text. This is a wonderful expression of worship in song. But whatever the text used, as long as it agrees with Scripture and is set to music that can edify, it will strengthen our faith when we express our hearts to God through corporate worship in song.

WORSHIP IN THE DANCE

Perhaps it is King David who most clearly demonstrated the propriety of dancing before the Lord. He danced with all his might, leading the Israelites in a procession when they brought the ark of the covenant back from captivity. (See 2 Samuel 6:14.) Willing to humble himself and lay aside his kingly robes, David danced with joy to celebrate the return of God's presence to His people.

Even the Book of Ecclesiastes declares that there is a time to dance. (See Ecclesiastes 3:4.) In contrast to most of the Canaanite dancing that was sensuous, lustful and performed for idolatrous festivals, the dancing of the Israelites was to be performed with joy, praise and as part of worship unto the Lord. Dancing before the Lord corporately is especially appropriate for occasions of rejoicing. When the children of Israel were delivered from Egypt, Miriam and the women danced and sang together to celebrate their great deliverance (Exod. 15:20–21). Nowhere does Scripture ever abolish or preclude the fact of dance as a proper expression of worship. In the Old Testament, there are numerous references to the dance, translated from many different Hebrew terms.

CLAPPING AND LIFTING UP OF HANDS

There are many references in the Scriptures to clapping and the lifting up of hands in praise and worship. It is unfortunate that many churches do not practice these biblical expressions of worship. Clapping our hands is a natural human response to joy and happiness. From the cradle, a baby learns to clap his or her hands in excited joyous response. The psalmist exhorts the people to this expression: "O clap your hands, all ye people" (Ps. 47:1). There is a wonderful release of praise and joy in our hearts when we give expression to it through clapping our hands.

The lifting up of our hands to God has great significance for the believer. The Scriptures teach that lifting our hands signifies several important aspects of worship: It is an act of surrender, a sign of taking a vow before the Lord and an appropriate expression in prayer and worship. Both the Old and the New Testaments give specific commands to raise our hands as an expression of worship:

> Let my prayer be set forth before thee as incense; and the lifting up of my hands as the evening sacrifice.
> —PSALM 141:2

> I will therefore that men pray every where, lifting up holy hands, without wrath and doubting.
> —1 TIMOTHY 2:8

When a congregation joins together in worship and lifts their hands in thanksgiving and surrender to the lordship of Christ, our hearts are released in a true worship expression that honors God and builds faith in the believer. Clapping our hands together releases a jubilant joy that laughs at the enemy and understands that Jesus has conquered every foe that would try to defeat us. These simple physical responses in corporate worship become powerful weapons in the expression of praise and worship that strengthen our faith.

SHOUT TO THE LORD

For many people, shouting has been reserved for ball games, where such excitement and "irreverence" is expected. Their sense of reverence for church would not allow them to raise their voices in a triumphant shout.

Nevertheless, the Scriptures do not merely *record* the shouts of God's people, such as those lifted up at the battle of Jericho; they *command* us to shout to the Lord with a voice of triumph. (See Psalm 47:1.)

One of the moods of the Holy Spirit is His conquering mood, in which He expresses joyful triumph over the enemy. I wrote in my book *Presenting the Holy Spirit:*

> When the Holy Spirit expresses Himself in the conquering mood, He is joyful, triumphant, and victorious. "For this purpose the Son of God was manifested, that He might destroy the works of the devil" (1 John 3:8). The original meaning of the Greek word used here for destroy is *lou.* It means that Jesus came to outdo, undo, and overdo everything the devil ever did. Truly understanding Jesus' ultimate triumph over evil makes us want to shout "Hallelujah!" When a person or a church realizes that kind of victory, the Holy Spirit is ready to rejoice as the conquering armies in Bible history did when they returned home with the spoils.[1]

Though there are times of worship during which we want simply to bow quietly in His presence, sensing the awe of His greatness and responding in quiet humility, there are other times when by the inspiration of the Holy Spirit congregations must express their jubilation and triumph with a shout to the Lord. Every biblical expression of worship has its place and can be cultivated for the building and edifying of the body of Christ.

Every expression of true worship will magnify God and strengthen the church when we learn to participate corporately in praise and worship. We do not need to be afraid of biblical expressions of worship as long as we use them to express our love and adoration for the King. No one should try to bring attention to himself by making unusual outbursts when a church is worshiping together. This does not bring glory to God but focuses attention on the person. But when a congregation is led in song, dance, lifting of hands, clapping or even shouting to the Lord, God receives glory, and true worship is experienced.

13

The Prophetic Power of Worship

Worship in the Coming Revival

IF, AS WE BELIEVE, WORSHIP IN SPIRIT AND IN TRUTH IS THE priority for every Christian and will be the central theme of mankind's relationship with God for eternity, it follows that whatever God does in the earth to bring revival must be characterized by pure spiritual worship.

The Spirit of God is continually seeking hearts that are willing to humble themselves to worship God in spirit and in truth. The Scriptures promise that those who seek God will find Him and, through worship, enjoy relationship with Him. That life-giving relationship will always involve our response to God in worship. The psalmist declared:

> I will praise the name of God with a song, and
> will magnify him with thanksgiving. This also
> shall please the LORD better than an ox or bullock
> that hath horns and hoofs. The humble shall see
> this, and be glad: and your heart shall live that
> seek God.
>
> —PSALM 69:30–32

From ancient times, the people of God knew that if they would seek Him earnestly He would reveal Himself to them. The Scriptures declare this truth in many places: "But if from thence thou shalt seek the LORD thy God, thou shalt find him, if thou seek him with all thy heart and with all thy soul" (Deut. 4:29). And always that seeking was motivated by love of the eternal God, who Himself is the essence of love. As the Shulamite maiden responded when she had lost her beloved, so does every heart that truly seeks to know Him: "I will rise now, and go about the city in the streets, and in the broad ways I will seek him whom my soul loveth" (Song of Sol. 3:2). Once we have experienced God's love, it is painful to think we would have to live without His wonderful presence.

We cannot overemphasize the fact that the deepest longing of mankind is to know love that can be experienced only through relationship with God. That relationship will be defined by our worship of Him. It is human destiny to worship the One who gave us the gift of life and who desires to fellowship with His creation. There is no hint of tyranny or selfishness in this divine order of God's relationship to mankind, as some have suggested. True revelation of the love of God to a human heart automatically evokes the deepest response of praise, gratitude and worship from the heart of His creation. Pure spiritual worship should be viewed not so much as a requirement for relationship with God but rather as the spontaneous response of a human heart that has touched the loving heart of God.

Reverence for God brings us into true worship. True worship also deepens our reverence for God. When we humble our hearts to seek God and experience the awesome manifest presence of God in worship, we are filled with a healthy fear of and reverence for Him. Our hearts cringe at the thought of anything that would displease Him when we bow before Him and pour out our hearts in love and adoration.

Whether we view worship through the eyes of the liturgy of the Promised Land, or John the Revelator's vision around the throne of God, or the exhilarating exhortations of the psalms to let everything that has breath praise the Lord, our hearts should be inspired to seek God. As we seek Him, we will experience the life-changing presence of God. We will discover our true destiny and enjoy fulfillment of our deepest human longing for relationship through worship.

We can live every day knowing our lives are fulfilling the purpose for which we were created when we make our worship top priority. Our personal destiny, which is by definition tied up in the ultimate destiny of the church, will be fulfilled as we grow in our worship relationship with God. All the divine promises given to the children of God can be realized only when we walk in fellowship with God and with one another. We should encourage one another to this end, learning to humble ourselves in worship so that we can become a people who will bring glory to God.

Worshiping hearts will touch the heart of God and express His desire for unity in the body of Christ, as well as His love for lost souls. True spiritual worship will cleanse our hearts from the pharisaical spirit that cannot go into the kingdom and also keeps others from entering. (See Matthew 23:13.) Religion is a poor substitute for relationship with a holy God. Theology, doctrine and tradition cannot change the heart of man, but only serve to puff him up in pride through knowledge about God. The worshiper who is humbled by his sin and who bows before God in deep contrition will find God's loving arms outstretched to forgive, cleanse and restore him to relationship with God.

As we are restored to the relationship with God for which we were created, we begin to see all of mankind through the loving eyes of Jesus, who gave His life that sinners might be reconciled to God. The wonder of His divine love not only deepens our worship of God personally but also strengthens our desire for fellowship with other believers. We discover a dynamic and power in our corporate expression of worship that we cannot experience even through our personal expression of worship. To become a part of a larger entity than ourselves is to discover the heart of God for community and fellowship as experienced within the Trinity: Father, Son and Holy Spirit.

When this priority of worship becomes the central focus of the church, we are going to see the great End-Time move of God that the Scriptures have prophesied. In order for worship to have its right priority, the church will have to experience deep repentance and brokenness and allow the Holy Spirit to cleanse us from all that has kept us from true spiritual worship. When the Holy Spirit shines His light on the truth of God's Word and we choose to obey Him completely, we are going to be delivered from the hindrances that keep us from worshiping in spirit and in truth.

When everything is in order, as it was in Israel when the glory of God fell, the church will be filled with the glory of God. That powerful manifest presence of God that filled David's tabernacle with joy and rejoicing, that prevented the priests in Solomon's temple from standing to minister and that characterized the day of Pentecost when the disciples were gathered together in one accord, is going to fill the church again as we learn to worship together in spirit and truth. The prophets did not declare in vain: "For the earth shall be filled with the knowledge of the glory of the LORD, as the waters cover the sea" (Hab. 2:14). God intends to fill the earth with His glory.

To believe otherwise would be to negate the prayer of Christ that will surely be answered:

> Neither pray I for these alone, but for them also which shall believe on me through their word; that they all may be one; as thou, Father, art in me, and I in thee, that they also may be one in us: that the world may believe that thou hast sent me. And the glory which thou gavest me I have given them; that they may be one, even as we are one: I in them, and thou in me, that they may be made perfect in one; and that the world may

know that thou hast sent me, and hast loved them, as thou hast loved me.

—JOHN 17:20–23

Jesus expressed the desire of the Father's heart to fill those who believed on Him with His glory and to show His love to the world through them. Unity would be the divine result of receiving His glory. All the human methods and good intentions of sincere Christians have not resulted in breaking down barriers of denominationalism, prejudice of race and gender and other hindrances to unity in the body of Christ. It will be the glory of God given to us as we behold Him in worship that will create the unity that will convince the world of God's love for them.

The apostle Paul declared, "But we all, with open face beholding as in a glass the glory of the Lord, are changed into the same image from glory to glory, even as by the Spirit of the Lord" (2 Cor. 3:18). Worship in spirit and in truth, beholding God as the Spirit of God reveals Him to us, will change us so that we bear the image of God and can be filled with His glory. Then we will exchange our prejudices and opinions, even our theology, for the longing of God's heart to fill His church with His glory and through it to display His love to the world.

I believe our priorities must agree with God's before we will be part of what He intends to do in the earth. Jack Hayford concurs:

> Even in the dark times, we must realize the vast power of worship to give our lives meaning and purpose. For one thing, bowing before any god

declares our values. If we surrender to the lying deity veiled in feelings of despair and aimlessness when they visit us, we will bow before hopelessness, exchanging the Almighty God for a lesser god. But worshiping God even amid despair is a way to defy the Adversary and declare our valuing of the good—the best—in life: The Lord! There is no more worthy purpose to praise; no more worthy time for it!

In worship we also name priorities. Putting God first enables us to focus on first things—His love, our blessings, our responsibility to others—instead of the temporary feelings of despair. Worship...even forms certain expectations so that our worship determines what we will yet discover in the future.[1]

What is the future of the church? Of your life as a believer? Is it dark and foreboding as the present world condition would make it seem? Worship in spirit and in truth will elevate our understanding and expectation of life in the future as well as in the present. Our future in God is filled with hope and promise for the life—the abundant life—Christ came to give to us. (See John 10:10.) We receive revelation of that hope through the Word and through true spiritual worship. "Defying the adversary," as Jack Hayford states it, by worshiping the true God will deliver us from the hopelessness of the world system that is under the influence of the devil himself.

Many years ago, when much of the church world was still living with an escapist mentality—hoping to just disappear one day in the Rapture—God sovereignly opened my mind and heart through a comprehensive vision of what He planned to do. He changed my understanding of the purpose of the church in the End Times. He showed me the great revival that was coming on the earth to fulfill the word of the prophets and the purposes of God. I understood what Joel saw when he declared, "And it shall come to pass afterward, that I will pour out my spirit upon all flesh; and your sons and your daughters shall prophesy, your old men shall dream dreams, your young men shall see visions: and also upon the servants and upon the handmaids in those days will I pour out my spirit" (Joel 2:28–29).

I began to preach the wonderful news of coming revival and of a great End-Time harvest of souls that God was going to bring into His kingdom worldwide. The churches where I ministered looked at me in disbelief, for I was contradicting everything their "escapist theology" had taught them. They were convinced that the world was going to get worse and worse and that the church in its powerlessness was going to have to endure the mess until Jesus came back to rescue them. That is not what the Bible teaches. According to the Scriptures, God is going to have a glorious church, without spot or wrinkle, and a bride that is worthy of His Son. (See Ephesians 5:27.)

In the vision God gave me, I saw a huge hydroelectric power plant held in the hands of Jesus. I understood that the power plant represented the church. The Holy Spirit showed me how carefully the divine workman was laying the foundations for that plant. He let me see all the intricacies of tubes and tubulars, primary and secondary lines—using terms that were unfamiliar to me—to show me His working in the earth. He was networking huge water lines from church to church where the water of the Word had found a reservoir in worshiping people. In my book *Stones of Remembrance,* I described the vision in detail:

> I understood that the water that would fill this great plant was the Word of God and that the power plant was the church. God showed me that the water of the Word left the throne of God and came down through time from the beginning of the church...I saw streams of truth that had left the throne, been dammed up by denominations, and the water had stopped running... In the vision God gave me He was building a new power plant, and this time it was going to be able to carry the water. The Holy Spirit spoke to me, "This time when I turn the switch, no devil, no demon, no man, or no denomination will ever be able to dam it up again."[2]

God filled my heart with certainty and expectation that He is going to send an old-fashioned, heaven-sent, sky-blue, sin-killing, gully-washing revival. This great End-Time revival is going to demolish the denominational pride that divides His church, as well as the prejudice, tradition, custom and culture that have kept the church from knowing the unity for which Christ died, the unity that will bring glory to God. As believers worship together in spirit and in truth, they are going to walk in fellowship with one another, allowing for differences of expression and even doctrinal emphasis, without breaking the unity of the Spirit. As we bow our hearts in pure spiritual worship, the glory of God is going to fill the earth as the waters cover the sea.

I believe such a revival is imminent. Indeed, in many parts of the earth, there is a great harvest of souls already pouring into the kingdom of God. And in our nation, large groups of believers from different denominational backgrounds are worshiping and fellowshiping together around the lordship of Jesus Christ. A great prayer movement in our country involving international leadership is helping to train believers in many aspects of intercession that will help to bring down strongholds over our nation and our cities and initiate reconciliation once again to God. This grassroots concern and involvement in prayer that is bringing unity among believers cannot be underestimated in its potential power for turning our nation from apostasy to great revival.

The true church in these days of testing and training is being transformed from pitiful impotence into a powerful influence in the earth as the Holy Spirit reveals Christ in His glory through the lives of believers. The church is going to move in power to bring people to Christ, the living Word. This glorious church will set the pace, demand respect and again hold a high reputation for godliness and holiness. It will be a remnant, not in the sense of a small number, but in the sense of being distinctive in character, separate from the false church. "Remnant" refers to a special people, protected from destruction. (See Zephaniah 2:7, 9; Revelation 12:17). As the glory of God shines through Christ's church, protecting her from destruction, she will be God's instrument to speak to the world before Christ's return.[3]

Our government, church denominations, social organizations, school systems and industries—which have become corrupt, motivated by self-promotion, serving for gold and silver and ruled by covetous practices—will all be changed by the power of God's divine presence. I believe this move of God will be so powerful that throughout our land we will see a return to the great historical foundations of this nation, which declare that in God we trust. People will again talk about God as our fathers did. Their conversations will concern the visitation of God rather than the Emmy awards. They will discuss "the riches of the glory of his inheritance in the saints" instead of bank accounts, interest rates and retirement programs (Eph. 1:18).[4]

Armed with a greater understanding of the centrality of pure spiritual worship to our individual lives and the corporate life of the church, we can choose to be a part of the great revival God is bringing to the earth. We must never take for granted that because we are born-again Christians we will be included in God's purposes for these last days. It is imperative that we humble ourselves to seek God, desiring to worship Him in spirit and in truth, in order to know His heart and be a part of His great plan for the End-Time harvest He desires. Pure spiritual worship will guarantee that the destiny for our lives and the church will be fulfilled in His time.

The Callings of God

For the gifts and callings of God are without repentance.

—ROMANS 11:29

1. **Called to fellowship with His Son**
   1 Corinthians 1:9
   1 John 1:6–7

2. **Called to peace**
   1 Corinthians 7:15

3. **Called into the grace of Christ**
   Galatians 1:6

4. **Calls His own sheep by name**
   John 10:3

5. **Called according to His purpose**
   Romans 8:28–30

6. **Called to lead the life He has imparted to us (or called to abide)**
   1 Corinthians 7:17–20

7. **Called unto liberty**
   Galatians 5:13

8. **Called to walk worthy of the vocation where-with we are called**
   Ephesians 4:1

9. **Called unto holiness**
   1 Thessalonians 4:7

10. **Called unto complete sanctification of spirit, soul and body**
    1 Thessalonians 5:23–24

11. **Called with a holy calling**
    2 Timothy 1:9

12. **Called to salvation through sanctification**
    2 Thessalonians 2:13–14

13. **Called out of darkness into His marvelous light**
    1 Peter 2:9

14. **Called to inherit a blessing**
    1 Peter 3:8–9

15. **Called to glory and virtue**
    2 Peter 1:3

16. **Called to the marriage supper and to be the bride who has made herself ready**
    Revelation 13:7–9

17. **Called to apostleship**
    Romans 1:5–6

18. **Called to be saints**
    Romans 1:7

19. **Called the foolish, weak and base things of the world**
    1 Corinthians 1:26–29

20. **Called of God to minister unto Him as priest**
    Hebrews 5:4–5

21. **That you may know what is the hope of His calling**
    Ephesians 1:17–23

22. **Give diligence to make your calling sure**
    2 Peter 1:10

23. **Called in one hope of your calling**
    Ephesians 4:4

24. **Called unto His kingdom and glory**
    1 Thessalonians 2:12

25. **Called in one body**
    Colossians 3:15

26. **Called to receive the promise of eternal inheritance**
    Hebrews 9:15

27. **The high calling of God in Christ Jesus**
    Philippians 3:14

28. **Called to suffer**
    1 Peter 1:20–21
    Romans 8:17
    2 Timothy 2:12

29. **Many are called, but few are chosen (few choose to respond to His call; therefore, they are not called "the chosen." They did not choose to be the called.)**
    Matthew 20:16
    Matthew 22:14

30. **Called to eternal life**
    1 Timothy 6:12

31. **Called to be justified and glorified**
    Romans 8:30

32. **Called to be vessels of mercy**
    Romans 9:23–24

33. **Called as sinners to repentance**
    Mark 2:17
    Luke 5:32
    Matthew 9:13

34. **Called out of Egypt**
    Matthew 2:15

35. **Called to be disciples**
    Mark 1:20

36. **Called to be conformed to the image of His Son**
    Romans 8:29

37. **Called to be His people, His chosen**
    Romans 9:25–26

38. **Called to obedience**
    Hebrews 11:8

39. Called to be with Him
Revelation 17:14

40. Called to humble ourselves, pray, seek His face and turn from our wicked ways
2 Chronicles 7:14

41. Called from our mother's womb
Isaiah 49:1

These callings come with an RSVP. Hearing and answering the calls are two different things. You have free volition in the matter. Remember, however, you either answer the callings, or you answer for them.

Notes

Chapter 1
The Priority of Worship

1. Clark Pinnock, *Flame of Love* (Downers Grove, IL: Intervarsity Press, 1996), 215.
2. Oswald Chambers, *The Best From All His Books, Vol. 1* (Nashville, TN: Oliver Nelson, 1987), 390.

Chapter 2
The Imperative of Worship

1. *International Standard Bible Encyclopaedia,* Electronic Database (Biblesoft, 1996).
2. *Adonai*—(a-do'-ni), (ad-o-na'-i) ('adhonay): A divine name, translated "Lord," and signifying, from its derivation, "sovereignty." Its vowels are found in the Massoretic Text with the unpronounceable tetragrammaton YHWH; when the Hebrew reader came to these letters, he always substituted in pronunciation the word "adhonay." Its vowels combined with the tetragrammaton form the word "Yahweh (Jehovah)." From *International Standard Bible Encyclopaedia,* Electronic Database (Biblesoft, 1996).
3. *International Standard Bible Encyclopaedia,* Electronic Database (Biblesoft, 1996).
4. Ibid.
5. Ibid.
6. Ibid.
7. Fuchsia Pickett, *God's Dream* (Shippensburg, PA: Destiny Image, 1993), 4–5.
8. Ibid., 6–7.

9. Fuchsia Pickett, *Presenting the Holy Spirit, Vol. 1* (Lake Mary, FL: Creation House, 1995), 4–6.
10. Ibid., 143–178.

CHAPTER 3
TRUE SPIRITUAL WORSHIP

1. Pickett, *God's Dream.* Dr. Pickett answers these questions as the thesis of the book.
2. *International Standard Bible Encyclopaedia,* Electronic Database (Biblesoft, 1996).
3. Ibid.
4. Ibid.
5. Ibid.

CHAPTER 4
REVERENCE TOWARD GOD

1. *Matthew Henry's Commentary on the Whole Bible: New Modern Edition,* Electronic Database (Hendrickson Publishers, Inc., 1991).

CHAPTER 5
FELLOWSHIP WITH GOD

1. Pickett, *Presenting the Holy Spirit, Vol. 1,* 83–84.

CHAPTER 6
WORSHIP IN THE OLD TESTAMENT

1. *The New Unger's Bible Dictionary* (Chicago: Moody Press, 1988).
2. Ibid.
3. Ibid.
4. Ibid.
5. Ibid.

6. Kevin J. Conner, *The Tabernacle of David* (Portland, OR: Bible Temple, Publishing, 1976), 37–40.
7. Ibid., 61–72.

Chapter 7
Worship in the Promised Land

1. *International Standard Bible Encyclopaedia*, Electronic Database (Biblesoft, 1996).

Chapter 9
The Dynamo of Praise

1. C. S. Lewis, *Reflections on the Psalms* (New York: Harcourt, Brace, 1958).
2. Ibid.

Chapter 10
The Value of Worship

1. Andrew Murray, *Abide in Christ* (Old Tappan, NJ: Fleming H. Revell, n.d.), 12.

Chapter 11
Hindrances to Worship

1. Fuchsia Pickett, *The Next Move of God* (Lake Mary, FL: Creation House, 1994), 70–77.

Chapter 12
Corporate Worship

1. Pickett, *Presenting the Holy Spirit, Vol. 1,* 156–157.

CHAPTER 13
PROPHETIC POWER OF WORSHIP

1. Jack Hayford, *The Heart of Praise* (Ventura, CA: Regal Books, 1992), 134–35.
2. Fuchsia Pickett, *Stones of Remembrance* (Lake Mary, FL: Creation Hous, 1997), 115–116, 118.
3. Pickett, *The Next Move of God*, 164–165.
4. Ibid., 173.